Cool Socks
Warm Feet

*Six Exceptional Sock Patterns
for Printed Yarns*

Lucy Neatby

Tradewind Knitwear Designs Inc.

Project management: Lynda Gemmell
Photography: Mary Bray
Cover design: John Emberson
Technical editor: Arden Okazaki
Copy editor: Don Evans
Design: Lynda Gemmell
Text copyright © 2003 Lucy Neatby
Photograph copyright © 2003 Mary Bray

TRADEWIND KNITWEAR DESIGNS

First published in Canada by Tradewind Knitwear Designs Inc.: October 2003.

Second Edition: January 2004. Third Edition: May 2006.

ISBN 0-9733940-0-5

Many of the techniques described in Lucy's patterns are demonstrated on her **Knitter's Companion** series of DVDs! Ask your local yarn store or visit www.lucyneatby.com

Contents

Acknowledgements

One pair of hands is never enough . . .

I would like to thank the following "knitbuddies" and the many students who have both collectively and individually prodded and poked, coaxed and cajoled me into both starting and persevering with this project.

Arden Okazaki, knitter, proof-reader extra-ordinaire and lynch-pin of the entire project has knit every sock and variant thereof and went wild with the mini-socks.

Corrie Watt, Susan Hannah and Karen Parusel, my Nova Scotian support team, have all contributed in more ways than I can say. Without them this publication would never have happened.

Susan Lucy, Bev Smith and Catherine Vardy generously gave knitting and technical support and convinced me that it could be done. Martina Robinson put temptation in my path by casually leaving a bag of delicious sock yarn for me to play with.

And lastly, in chronology only, Lynda Gemmell (also a Cabin Fever designer), who said she could put it all together and make it look and behave like a book. She has been unfailingly encouraging and cheery, even at times when I could not bear to think about another sock!

The techniques you will read about in this book
may also be seen demonstrated by me
(pink hair and all!) on my DVD series
Lucy Neatby - A Knitter's Companion
Sock Knitting Techniques 1 & 2.

Introduction

This select collection of six sock patterns was inspired by the superabundance of wild new sock yarns which knit to gauges of 6.5 - 9 stitches per inch. This vogue for printed yarns offers far more in the way of colour variety within a single filament of yarn than knitters, other than hand-spinners or artful dyers, have previously experienced. The excitement of reaching a new colour development in the yarn is an added incentive to knit "just a little more," to see what is going to happen next. It's harder than ever to put down your knitting.

When the fascination and magic of sock knitting are coupled with colour excitement, you have an infinite source of delight. The pleasure in watching a fully formed sock grow off your needles should be experienced by every knitter.

The simple yet sublime socks presented in this book are designed to show off the colours in the yarns, yet offer the knitter more than an endless repetition of a basic sock pattern. The independently-minded, multi-colour yarns tend not to show off cables, lace or complex stranded (two-colours-per round) patterns to their best advantage, so these have largely been avoided.

However, a variety of styles of heels, toes and cast-on methods is offered.

Great knitting is a sum of small parts. At first glance, some of these socks may not look particularly revolutionary, except for their colours, but they are full of small details that add up to very special socks. These patterns contain useful techniques which may enhance your pleasure, not only in knitting socks, but in other areas of your knitting life.

Miniaturization details are offered for those who would like to try all the techniques on a small scale.

Lastly, there are suggestions on taking various elements from different patterns and combining them to make unique, hybrid socks of your own.

You may not ever sit down and read this volume from cover to cover, but there is information for you to dip in, dabble with and explore, as the need, or inclination arises.

May your socks be a joy to knit, wear or bestow. *Happy knitting.*

Assumptions

Certain customary assumptions have been made in writing this book. It is assumed that the knitter is working the stitches from the left needle to the right, and that the stitches lie on the needles with the leading edge at the front of the needle. A knit stitch is created by placing the right-hand needle into a stitch to the left of the yarn at the front of the needle. Beginning with the yarn away from the knitter, the yarn is brought up between the needles and away to the back again. For a purl stitch, the needle enters the stitch from the right (needle-tip to needle-tip); with the yarn forward towards the knitter, the yarn is thrown over the right-hand needle and down between both.

Incidentally, please note that it makes no difference to your knitting which hand you favour to manipulate your working yarn. It is the direction of the yarn around the needle that is important.

Where the term "work" is given, it is intended that you should knit or purl the stitch(es) as is appropriate for your established pattern. The terms "cast off" and "bind off" are equivalent.

Alternative Knitters

There are a myriad of methods of knitting. The direction of working, the direction of throwing the yarn or the direction of entering a stitch may vary; none is wrong, provided you achieve the results you desire and can control the gauge of your fabric. Knitting directions and abbreviations make assumptions; thus, for many knitters, k2t (knit two stitches together) will give a one-stitch decrease which slopes / (to the right). However, if you throw your yarn in an alternative direction or your stitches lie on the needle with the trailing edge in front, knitting two stitches together will not necessarily give you the desired slope of decrease. For this reason, the desired effect of an abbreviation has been given in its definition; if you have to work a k2t tbl to achieve an untwisted, / (right sloping) decrease, then so be it!

It's *your* knitting; make it do your bidding.

Tips for Great Socks

If you haven't time to read the rest of this book, just scan these few points!

1. For sock knitting, use as small a needle size as you comfortably can. The firmer the fabric produced, the longer the sock will last. It will wear well and recover its shape after washing, donning or doffing.

2. When working in the round with double-pointed needles (dpns), help to avoid baggy or laddered "corners" by moving or circulating your stitches around at your convenience. This is easiest on a set of five needles. When a needle is empty, work an extra one or two stitches onto the old working needle as before (only four needles working at this point), then introduce the empty needle and proceed as usual. This may be repeated each time a needle is empty. It is not compulsory to have equal numbers of stitches on all needles at all times. Markers can be used to keep track of important positions in the round. If necessary, stitches may also be slipped unworked from one needle to another; on some occasions, this may be made easier by using an extra needle.

3. The short rows for turning the Common Heel are worked in plain stocking stitch. This is a thin fabric for one of the areas of heaviest wear in the whole sock. Make it more durable by adding a reinforcing yarn (woolly nylon or fine mohair) to your working yarn or by weaving in another yarn at the back of the work or by using two yarns in an alternating "salt and pepper" pattern. (Use both ends of the same ball for single-colour socks.) The toe may be reinforced similarly.

4. For peace of mind and fine fit, you can try the sock on at any stage. Slip the stitches onto a length of yarn and pop the sock on.

5. Work as near the tips of your needles as possible, but always form the stitch on the full width of the needle. Avoid stretching the adjacent stitches apart as you work them.

6. It is easier to work ribbing or textured patterns if you arrange the stitches so that each needle begins with a knit stitch. Arrange the stitches accordingly. It is not vital to have the same number of stitches on each needle at all times.

7. Smaller size needles are rarely necessary for a sock rib. The needles chosen to give a

durable fabric are finer than would customarily be used for the given weight of yarn and will therefore be suitable for the rib.

8. As you cast on, make a conscious effort to space each new stitch a little further apart from its neighbour than usual. This will give the cast-on edge considerably improved elasticity.

9. When working with very few stitches, keeping only three needles in the work will make things more stable. A double-knit tube (the stitches of both layers of the tube are worked from a single needle) is also an alternative.

10. Use as many markers as necessary to help you keep your orientation. This is of particular importance when you are circulating your stitches from one needle to another. Consider using different coloured yarns to mark the beginning/end of the round, decrease positions, and other significant spots. Try using Running Yarn Markers (page 113). They do not drop off the needles when they fall at the junction between two needles, or clutter up the knitting, and can be made from scraps of surplus yarn.

11. To avoid having to move the markers constantly, mark lines of decreases thus: place markers *after* k2t decreases (for example, knit to 3 stitches before marker, end k2t, k1) and *before* ssk decreases (after marker k1, ssk, knit to end).

12. The joggle in the cast-on edge may be smoothed when finishing the sock by easing any excessive slack into the adjacent stitches, followed by a careful darn with the cast-on tail. Or, when casting on, by adding one extra stitch. Pass this extra stitch over the first stitch before commencing the first round.

13. If desperate for needles, the deliberate use of an odd pin won't hurt. It is also a subtle method of changing gauge, as the odd pin will only be used every fifth needle and will move around the tube evenly.

14. To reduce the possibility of puckers and incremental gathering-in of the sock once two-colour-per-round knitting starts, invert the sock on the needle. The private side of the sock will now be facing outwards, but you will still be working exactly as usual and able to see the public side of the fabric as you knit. The floats between the stitches can no longer jump across the corners; they have no option but to go around the exterior of the fabric.

15. When commencing a complex pattern, it is handy to insert one round of plain knitting prior to the patterning. This will be virtually invisible and a useful escape route should the top need subsequent surgery.

16. When joining a new ball of variegated yarn mid-project, you may like to wind into your new ball of yarn so it begins at the same point in the sequence where the old yarn ceased. To avoid reversing the sequence, work the yarn from the same end of the ball.

17. Always check the fibre blend information and washing instructions on the ball bands.

18. To test the squareness of the heel flap, at the end of a heel flap row, fold the flap diagonally. If the needle lies parallel to the side of the flap with no extra heel flap showing, you have a square. Keep going — don't skimp on it.

Helpful Notes

Throughout the pattern instructions, *Cool Socks Warm Feet* offers pertinent information in the form of references to tips and techniques, and pattern-specific notes. The following additional information applies to all the patterns.

Yarn Selection

The weights and colours of the yarns suitable for any of the patterns in this book are many and various. Some of the smaller-stitch-number socks will adapt perfectly to large-size socks if worked in a heavier yarn. Check your gauge and required ankle measurement!

Any specific colour sequence requirements are given in the individual pattern and obviously, you may work any of these socks in single-colour yarns.

Wraps Per Inch

An approach to measuring yarn favoured by spinners is to measure "wraps per inch." Wind a length of the chosen yarn *gently* around a ruler, slide the strands side by side with each other, but do not compress them. Count how many wraps cover one inch in ruler length.

Needles

These patterns are written assuming that the knitter is using a set of five needles, however, with the aid of markers to differentiate the various sections of the sock, you may also employ single or multiple flexible circular needles.

Suggested needle/stitch allocations have been given in each pattern to aid the knitting-up of new stitches after turning the heel and other action-packed areas. Once you clearly see the decrease positions, resume circulating the groups of stitches. *See Tip #2, page 7.* Allow yourself a couple of rounds to establish the decrease positions, or place markers in the reference positions and move your stitches with wild abandon. *See Tips #10 and #11, page 8.*

Swatching and Gauge

Please swatch! It's your only guide to size. Ideally, the swatch should be laundered and blocked prior to taking measurements. These socks work best at gauges between 6.5 - 9 stitches per inch.

Sizing Your Socks

Socks should be sized based on real body measurements. Shoe size has little to do with sizing socks. Shoe size and ankle measurements have no exact relationship either. To knit a well-tailored sock, take or request (if knitting for absent feet) the ankle circumference (just above the joint), the exact foot length (not shoe length), and, for even more precision, a measurement around the foot after the arch and just before the toes. This measurement is usually very close to the ankle measurement and sock patterns assume it to be so. In the event of a difference of more than ¼", *see Instep Decreases, page 95.*

Among veteran sock knitters you will hear people say, "I always knit a 68-stitch sock." What they are not saying out loud is that they have a favourite needle size and a favourite sock yarn, both of which they use regularly, and they have found this combination to work very well for them. Their initial swatches (or days of producing ill-fitting socks) are distant history. Now they swatch mentally.

For example, I can predict that a sock worked in certain yarns in a single colour with 76 stitches will fit me nicely. If the pattern is two colours per round, but all other factors remain the same, I'll knit with 80 stitches. Alternatively, I could use the next larger needle size and stick with 76 stitches.

As knitting is so delightfully elastic, round down the number of stitches calculated by the gauge x ankle measurement equation to the nearest given figure. For clingy patterns such as rib, or slightly less elastic fabrics (cables or two colours per round), round the numbers up.

The length of the sock is not entirely dependent on the length of the tube between the heel and the toe. The last knit of these (whether this is the toe or the Turkish heel), may need a little adjustment in the rate of shaping to fine tune the length. Try on or re-measure the sock before completing the graft. A sock should usually be about a third of an inch shorter than the extreme foot length.

Pattern Size Ranges

The patterns in *Cool Socks Warm Feet* have been given in a wide range of sizes, shown as #1 (#2, **#3**, #4, **#5**, #6, **#7**, #8, **#9**, #10). The miniature sock information is indicated by the use of squigily brackets { }. The term size does not in any instance relate to shoe size. Each size is a specific set of stitch numbers to allow you to use a variety of yarn weights and still be able to fit a wide range of human ankles. In fine weight yarn, a sock for a slender-ankled soul will be one of the smaller stitch numbers. In a DK or sport weight yarn, a sturdily shanked recipient will need a sock in the same stitch range.

If your size is shown in **bold**, it will remain so throughout. To avoid confusion, you may wish to highlight the stitch numbers that refer to your size throughout the pattern.

The pattern may have an apparently astronomical number of stitches for a mere sock. This is to enable you to knit at a fine gauge and still have a sock large enough to fit a real human foot.

Choose the size you wish to knit based on the ankle measurement in inches x gauge in stitches/inch.

For peace of mind and fine fit, try your sock on regularly. Slip the stitches onto a piece of yarn for the most accurate information. If you just hate swatching or for some other bizarre reason end up with an ill-fitting sock, there are a number of options open to you:

- Try making adjustments to the second sock based on the information contained in the first sock. Please don't immediately rip back the first sock — you will lose all the data on which to base your adjustments. Besides, you'll waste a perfectly good sock, albeit for a foot other than the one originally intended. Once you have one sock that fits, make a note of the relevant information. You can either rework the first sock, or knit another to match the first and you'll have a spare set for a deserving pair of naked feet.

- Single socks, mounted on an L-shaped form, make very attractive wall decorations. It is also not compulsory to make two identical socks. It does depend on how symmetrical you need to be, but socks with a family resemblance can be rather fun and help overcome the "second sock" syndrome from which some knitters suffer.

Sock Patterns

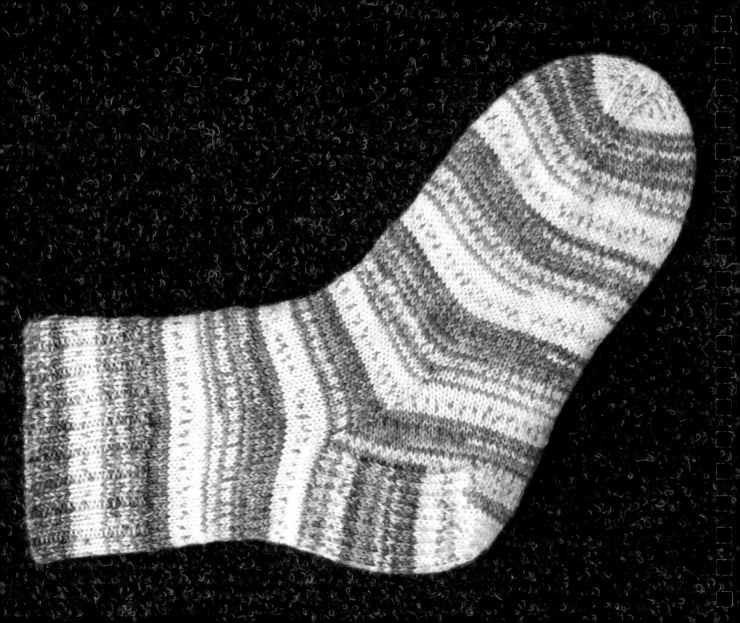

Simply Splendid Socks

Here is a pattern for a traditional, stocking stitch ankle sock. It comes with variations galore! For additional methods to adjust the fit of this sock, refer to *Sock Fit and Adjustment, page 93*. Shown above with a Tubular Cast-on for 2 x 2 Rib and Stocking Stitch Toe.

Yarn:
Fingering weight sock yarn, 50 g = approximately 160-212 m/175-230 yds. Approximately 12-15 wraps per inch.
A plain pair of ankle-length socks in the smaller sizes will require 100 g. For very long feet, larger ankle sizes or extended sock legs, allow extra yarn if using one of the shorter yardage yarns.

Gauge:
For a sock to wear well, it is important to knit a dense fabric. Take your chosen yarn and work a stocking stitch swatch 30 stitches wide on fine needles. Work on the finest size needles that you find comfortable. Once you have settled on a suitable gauge, measure the number of stitches per inch you are achieving; do not round off any fractions of stitches.

Needles:
A set of five, 2-2.75 mm (US # 0-2) double-pointed needles, 6-8" in length.

Size:
Measure ankle circumference (just above the joint), in inches.

How Many Stitches Do I Need?
Multiply your stitches/inch gauge figure by the ankle measurement in inches. Example at 7.75 sts per inch with a 9½" ankle = 73.62 sts. Round the figure down to the nearest multiple of 4 (in this case 72 sts).

Sock Cuff
Onto gauge-size dpns, using your regular method or Channel Island method, *see page 108,* cast on gently, 52 (56, **60**, 64, **68**, 72, **76**, 80, **84**, 88) {24} sts.

It is important that this edge has sufficient elasticity to stretch around the instep when putting on the sock, *see Tip #8, page 8.*

Round 1: (K1, p1), repeat to end of round. Place a marker at the begin-

Level: Beginner

ning/end point of the round, *see Tips #2, #6 and #10, pages 7, 8.*

Repeat Round 1 until at least 1½" {½"} of ribbing has been worked.

Next Round: Change to stocking stitch (every round knit). Work until the leg is the desired length, approximately 3-4" {1-2"} long. Stop at marker.

Knit the first quarter of the next round, 13 (14, **15**, 16, **17**, 18, **19**, 20, **21**, 22) {6} stitches. Turn.

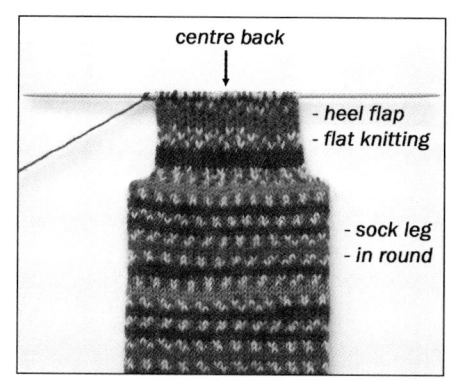

Photograph of a heel flap in progress.

Common Heel - Heel Flap

Row 1: (WS) (S1, p1) 13 (14, **15**, 16, **17**, 18, **19**, 20, **21**, 22) {6} times onto one dpn. Turn.

The heel flap is worked back and forth on these 26 (28, **30**, 32, **34**, 36, **38**, 40, **42**, 44) {12} stitches only.

Thread the remaining stitches (half of the original number) onto a piece of smooth yarn or holder; these will later form the **Instep**.

Row 2: (RS) S1, k25 (27, **29**, 31, **33**, 35, **37**, 39, **41**, 43) {11}.

Repeat these two rows until the heel flap is as long as it is wide, ending with a WS row. Fold the flap on a diagonal to check. See *Tip #18, page 9.*

Approximately 37 (39, **41**, 43, **45**, 47, **49**, 51, **53**, 55) {15} rows.

Turning the Heel

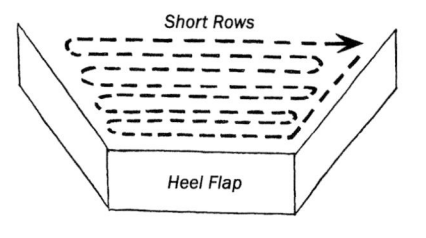

Diagram 1 illustrates the path of the yarn when working the short rows.

Row 1: (RS) S1, k18 (18, **20**, 20, **22**, 22, **24**, 24, **26**, 26) {6}, ssk, k1. Turn.

4 (6, **6**, 8, **8**, 10, **10**, 12, **12**, 14) {2} stitches remain unworked on LHN.

Row 2: (WS) S1, p 13 (11, **13**, 11, **13**, 11, **13**, 11, **13**, 11) {3}, p2t, p1. Turn.

4 (6, **6**, 8, **8**, 10, **10**, 12, **12**, 14) {2} stitches remain unworked on LHN.

With each successive pair of turning rows there will be two fewer unworked stitches on each needle. At the completion of each WS turning row the number of unworked stitches should be equal at either side.

Row 3: S1, k14 (12, **14**, 12, **14**, 12, **14**, 12, **14**, 12) {4}, ssk, k1. Turn.

Row 4: S1, p15 (13, **15**, 13, **15**, 13, **15**, 13, **15**, 13) {5}, p2t, p1. Turn. {Mini heel complete, 8 stitches remain.}

Row 5: S1, k16 (14, **16**, 14, **16**, 14, **16**, 14, **16**, 14), ssk, k1. Turn.

Row 6: S1, p17 (15, **17**, 15, **17**, 15, **17**, 15, **17**, 15), p2t, p1. Turn. #1 heel complete, 20 stitches remain.

*Sizes: #2 (**#3**, #4, **#5**, #6, **#7**, #8, **#9**, #10) only.*

Row 7: S1, k16 (**18**, 16, **18**, 16, **18**, 16, **18**, 16), ssk, k1. Turn.

Row 8: S1, p17 (**19**, 17, **19**, 17, **19**, 17, **19**, 17), p2t, p1. Turn. #2 & #3 heel complete, 20 (22) stitches remain.

*Sizes: #4 (**#5**, #6, **#7**, #8, **#9**, #10) only.*

Row 9: S1, k18 (**20**, 18, **20**, 18, **20**, 18), ssk, k1. Turn.

Row 10: S1, p19 (**21**, 19, **21**, 19, **21**, 19), p2t, p1. Turn. #4 & **#5** heel complete. 22 (24) stitches remain.

*Sizes: #6 (**#7**, #8, **#9**, #10) only.*

Row 11: S1, k20 (**22**, 20, **22**, 20), ssk, k1. Turn.

Row 12: S1, p21 (**23**, 21, **23**, 21), p2t, p1. Turn. #6 & #7 heel complete. 24 (26) stitches remain.

*Sizes: # 8 (**#9**, #10) only.*

Row 13: S1, k22, (**24**, 22), ssk, k1. Turn.

Row 14: S1, p23, (**25**, 23), p2t, p1. Turn. #8 & **#9** heel complete. 26 (28) stitches remain.

Size #10 only.

Row 15: S1, k24, ssk, k1. Turn.

Row 16: S1, p25, p2t, p1. Turn. #10 heel complete. 28 stitches remain.

All sizes: These remaining stitches now become the **Sole** stitches. Replace the **Instep** stitches onto a needle.

Knit Up Round - knitting in the round is re-established.

With RS facing:

Needle #1: S1, k19 (19, **21**, 21, **23**, 23, **25**, 25, **27**, 27) {7} across sole stitches.

Needle #2: Knit up 19 (20, **21**, 22, **23**, 24, **25**, 26, **27**, 28) {8} stitches by working into the back of the outer side of each of the slipped edge stitches along the right-hand side of the heel flap. *Working into the back of these stitches causes them to twist and prevents gaps. If your heel flap has more or fewer rows than the number specified, you will have a different number of stitches on Needles 2 and 4. Proceed as given but ignore the total stitch count.*

All sizes: work first 4 Instep stitches onto Needle #2. Total 23 (24, **25**, 26, **27**, 28, **29**, 30, **31**, 32) {12} stitches.

Needle #3: Knit across the next 18 (20, **22**, 24, **26**, 28, **30**, 32, **34**, 36) {4} Instep stitches (from holder).

Needle #4: Knit last 4 Instep stitches, knit up stitches along the left-hand side of the heel flap as Needle #2.

Needles #2 and #4 should have the same number of stitches.

Count your total stitches 84 (88, **94**, 98, **104**, 108, **114**, 118, **124**, 128) {36}. Place marker.

Foot Decrease Round: Knit across Needle #1. Knit until 5 stitches before the end of Needle #2, end

k2t, k3. Knit across Needle #3. Knit first 3 stitches of Needle #4, ssk, knit to end of round.

Repeat this round until the original number of stitches cast on is reached. 52 (56, **60**, 64, **68**, 72, **76**, 80, **84**, 88) {24} stitches.

Work on these stitches without shaping, until the sock is approximately 1¼-1½" {½"} short of the desired foot length.

Stocking Stitch Common Wedge Toe

Move the beginning-of-round marker to the mid-point of the sole.

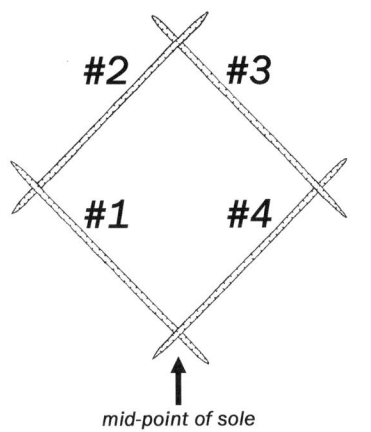

mid-point of sole

Diagram 2 illustrates the needle layout for the toe.

Rearrange the stitches on the needles, dividing the stitches into a quarter per needle from this marked position, 13 (14, **15**, 16, **17**, 18, **19**, 20, **21**, 22) {6} stitches.

The Simply Splendid Sock with Channel Island Cast-On and 1 x 1 Rib Cuff.

Toe Decrease Round

Needle #1: Knit to last 3 stitches, k2t, k1.

Needle # 2: K1, ssk, knit to end.

Repeat across Needle #3 and #4.

Work alternate plain knit and decrease rounds initially (for approximately 8 rounds) and then decrease every round until 16-20 {12} stitches remain.

Try the sock on regularly for the best possible fit. *For easiest grafting, complete the sock at the end of Needle #1 (the side of the sock), including the customary decrease. This gives two smooth rows of stitches to graft. See Diagram 3 below.*

Finishing

Graft the toe stitches together, neaten the small gaps at either side of the Instep and darn in all the ends. *See page 98 for sock finishing techniques.*

Variations

Once you have become comfortable with the structure of this type of sock, the variations are limitless. Ribbing is not compulsory! Non-curling stitch patterns are popular, but reverse stocking stitch "rolls" also make an attractive top. Stitch patterns with widthwise stretch and recovery properties are desirable.

The simplest colour variation is to work the cuffs, heel flap and toe in a contrasting colour. Two-row stripes are also easy and spectacular and the yarn may be stranded from stripe to stripe over 2-3 rounds without difficulty.

Solid-coloured yarns give interesting results when alternated with variegated yarns. Experiment with yarns having a colour in common, to give subtle irregular stripes; or use a strongly contrasting pair for a distinct pattern.

Diagram 3 illustrates grafting uneven numbers of stitches.

Can you spot the cables and the lurking lace?

Textured patterns are effectively hidden by the colourful yarn, see page 89.

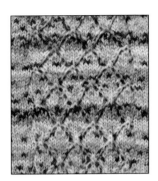

Odds and Socks!

A few detail shots of miscelleneous minutia.

Reverse Stocking Stitch ridges, made whenever two rounds of black yarn coincided, see page 92.

Textured Chequerboard determined by the colours in the yarn, see page 92.

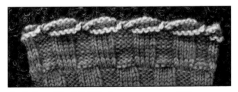

Latvian Twist Edging, see page 73.

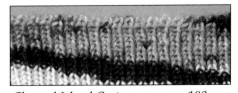

Channel Island Cast-on, see page 108.

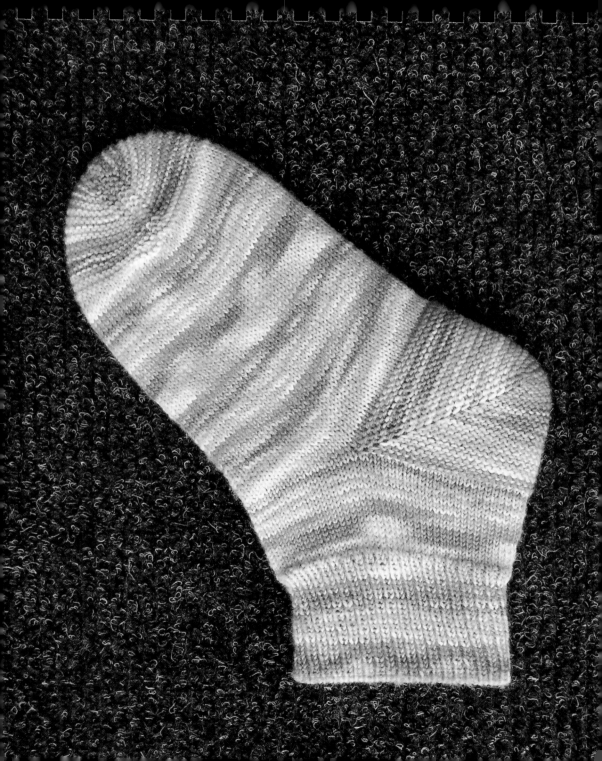

Timberline Toes

This practical sock is worked top-down from a Tubular Cast-On for 1 x 1 Rib to give a smooth, rounded edge with great elasticity. The Garter Stitch Toe and Short Row Heel (as shown) give a snug fit and add durability.

Yarn:
Fingering weight sock yarn, 50 g = approximately 160-212 m/175-230 yds. Approximately 12-15 wraps per inch.
A plain pair of ankle length socks in the smaller sizes will require 100 g. For very long feet, larger ankle sizes or extended sock legs, allow extra yarn if using one of the shorter yardage yarns.

Gauge:
For a sock to wear well, it is important to knit a dense fabric. Take your chosen yarn and work a stocking stitch swatch 30 stitches wide on fine needles. Work on the finest size needles that you find comfortable. Once you have settled on a suitable gauge, measure the number of stitches per inch you are achieving; do not round off any fractions of stitches.

Needles:
A set of five, 2-2.75 mm (US # 0-2) double-pointed needles and a second set of dpns, at least three sizes larger, for the Tubular Cast-On. Both sets of needles should be 6-8" in length. For example, gauge needle size 2 mm (US #0) partnered with larger size 3 mm (US #3).

Size:
Measure ankle circumference (just above the joint), in inches.

How Many Stitches Do I Need?
Multiply your stitches/inch gauge figure by the ankle measurement in inches. Example at 7.5 sts per inch with a 9¾" ankle = 73.125 sts. Round the figure down to the nearest multiple of 4 (in this case 72 sts).

Sock Cuff - Tubular or Plain

For Tubular: Onto a single dpn, three sizes larger than chosen gauge size, with similar weight, brightly contrasting WY and using Provisional Crochet method, *see page 110,* cast on 26 (28, **30**, 32, **34**, 36, **38**, 40, **42**, 44) {12} stitches *(half the total number of stitches for your size).*

For Plain: Cast on 52 (56, **60**, 64, **68**, 72, **76**, 80, **84**, 88) {24} stitches and proceed from Round 5.

Level: Intermediate

Round 1: With Main yarn and still using the **larger** needles, knit into the provisional stitches, working them onto 3 or 4 needles in preparation for knitting in the round.

Rounds 2 & 3: Join into the round now (checking for twists); knit 2 rounds on the **larger** needles. Place a marker at the end point of the round. *See Tip #10.* Introduce the fourth needle if not already in use.

Round 4: Introducing **gauge size** needles as you work, k1, wyif roll the cast on edge up behind the work and lift up the bar of Main yarn that lies between the bases of the first and second original stitches, and purl into this bar, (k1, purl into the next bar between the cast on stitches). *After the last true stitch has been worked, place the Main yarn tail over LHN from back to front and under the needle to the back again, hold it so; purl into the resulting "O" to create the final purl stitch.* This scraggy stitch will neaten beautifully later, using the tail.

52 (56, **60**, 64, **68**, 72, **76**, 80, **84**, 88) {24} sts.

Round 5: (K1, p1) to end of round. Repeat Round 5 six times, before **checking that your Tubular Cast-on unravels correctly**, leaving a beautiful edge. *While it is unlikely that you will encounter a problem with this edge, it is better to discover it now, rather than after the sock is complete.*

Continue in rib as set in Round 5 until at least 1½" {½"} of ribbing has been worked, or you can stand it no longer!

Now begin working in stocking stitch (knit every round) until the sock leg is the desired length, approximately 4" {1½"} long.

Stop 16 (17, **18**, 19, **20**, 21, **23**, 24, **25**, 26) {7} stitches before marker (30% of the round).

Garter Stitch Short Row Heel shown here in a Timberline sock.

Garter Stitch Short Row Heel

The heel, as given, is set in over 60% of the original number of sock stitches. This suits the majority of ankles, including those with high insteps or favouring a fuller heel.

(For those with incredibly slender ankles and dainty feet, adjust the figures to stop at 25% of the round before the marker.)

Use a new piece of yarn for the heel — even if you do not wish the heel to contrast — or change to a contrast colour. DO NOT cut off the Main working yarn. *If you have only one ball of yarn, use the opposite end to the one you are working from, for the duration of the heel. The separate heel yarn will give the neatest possible heel corners.*

Link the tail of the new yarn around the former working yarn; then, as you knit the first stitches of the heel, you may weave in the tail of the heel yarn at the back of the work, thus simultaneously preventing a future gap and neatening the tail.

With the new piece of heel yarn, knit the first half of the Heel stitches [16 (17, **18**, 19, **20**, 21, **23**, 24, **25**, 26) {7} stitches] onto an empty needle, the second half less one onto another needle [15 (16, **17**, 18, **19**, 20, **22**, 23, **24**, 25) {6} stitches], s1, bring the yarn between the needles, return the slipped stitch to the adjacent needle (next to the Instep stitches). This stitch has a "wrap" of the heel yarn around its base but remains in the Main colour.

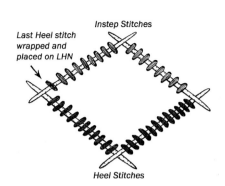

Instep Stitches
Last Heel stitch wrapped and placed on LHN
Heel Stitches

Diagram #4 shows the remaining 40% of the stitches (the Instep) divided onto two needles along with the one "wrapped" Heel stitch. Heel stitches are shown darkened for clarity.

Turn the work around, WS facing. With an empty needle, knit until only the first Heel stitch remains unworked [k30 (32, **34**, 36, **38**, 40, **44**, 46, **48**, 50) {12} stitches], s1, bring the yarn between the needles, return the slipped stitch to the adjacent needle holding the Instep stitches.

Subsequent Right and Wrong Side Rows: Turn the work RS facing, knit until one Heel stitch remains unworked on LHN [k29 (31, **33**, 35, **37**, 39, **43**, 45, **47**, 49) {11} stitches], SWR.

Turn the work WS facing, knit until one Heel stitch remains unworked on LHN [k28 (30, **32**, 34, **36**, 38, **42**, 44, **46**, 48) {10} stitches], SWR.

As an aid to keeping on track, there should always be the same number of "wrapped" stitches on either side of the heel on the completion of each WS row. Remember that the first "wrapped" stitch on the LHS will remain in the sock colour.

Repeat these two rows, ending with a WS row, approximately [k6 (6, **6**, 6, **8**, 8, **8**, 8, **8**, 8) {2}, SWR] or until the heel is deep enough for your foot. There should be an equal number of "wrapped" stitches on either side of the central 6 or 8 {2} stitches.

Suggested Stitch Distribution

Initially, when working the heel stitches on two dpns, on both RS and WS rows, knit two extra stitches onto the old needle before introducing the empty needle. *This staggers the junction of the work and helps to prevent distortion down the centre-line of the heel.*

When the number of working heel stitches is sufficiently reduced, work them onto a single needle, and use the spare needle to hold the middle section of the Instep stitches. This greatly increases working comfort.

Heel Increase Section

With RS Facing: Knit an equal number of stitches as in the previous row [k6 (6, **6**, 6, **8**, 8, **8**, 8, **8**, 8) {2} stitches], knit 1 previously "wrapped" stitch from the next needle. *Work this stitch as usual, leaving the "wrap" around the base of the stitch – don't knit into the wrap.* Slip the next heel stitch from the Instep needle to the RHN, bring the yarn between the needles (making a wrap) and return it to the Instep needle. Turn.

With WS Facing: Knit across all the stitches on the heel needles [k7 (7, **7**, 7, **9**, 9, **9**, 9, **9**, 9) {3} stitches], knit 1 previously "wrapped" stitch from the next needle – work the stitch as usual, SWR. Turn.

With RS Facing: Knit across all the stitches on the heel needles [k8 (8, **8**, 8, **10**, 10, **10**, 10, **10**, 10) {4} stitches], knit 1 previously "wrapped" stitch from the next needle - work the stitch as usual, SWR. Turn.

Repeat these two rows, increasing by one the number of stitches worked on each successive row, until the last heel stitch has received its second wrap. End with a WS row [k29 (31, **33**, 35, **37**, 39, **43**, 45, **47**, 49) {11} plus 1 previously "wrapped" stitch], wrap the heel yarn around the first heel stitch, but do not return the wrapped stitch to the LHN. Turn. Cut off the heel yarn, leaving a tail.

Resuming with the Main working yarn, tighten up any slack that has crept into the last stitch worked in the Main yarn, and knit across to the last heel stitches. The tail of the heel yarn may be woven in as you go. From the final stitch onwards, continue in stocking stitch (knit). Work on these stitches until the sock is approximately 1½" {½"} short of the desired foot length.

Garter Stitch Common Wedge Toe

Move the beginning-of-round marker to the side of the foot at a point that is a quarter of the total stitches beyond the mid-point of the sole. Place a second marker at the opposite side. Rearrange the stitches on the needles, dividing the stitches a quarter per needle, from the initial marked position [13 (14, **15**, 16, **17**, 18, **19**, 20, **21**, 22) {6} stitches per needle]. {See *page 62*}.

Round 1: (K1, ssk, knit to 3 stitches before the side marker, k2t, k1) twice.
Round 2: Purl.
Round 3: Knit.
Round 4: Purl.
Repeat Rounds 1-4 twice, followed by Rounds 1 and 2 only, until the toe is nearly long enough.

More frequent decreases are now required; substitute [(P1, ssp, purl to 3 stitches before the side marker, p2t, p1) twice] in place of Round 2. Try on the sock regularly to get the best possible fit.

Timberline Toes Sock with Garter Stitch Common Wedge Toe.

Complete the sock at the marker at the end of a purl round, with 16 to 20 stitches remaining.

Finishing

Graft the toe stitches together, reinforce the stitches on either side of the heel and darn in all the ends. *See page 98 for sock finishing techniques.*

Variations

A plain stocking stitch toe may be substituted. Work knit rounds in place of the purl rounds, and shape more frequently.

Crenellated Toe-Up Socks

These socks use a Bosnian-style, Square Garter Stitch Toe and a Turkish Heel. Beginning at the toe has many advantages: custom fit, last minute size adjustments and, for your peace of mind, the option, once past the ankle, of continuing to work up the leg until you have used up almost half of the yarn and know that you have sufficient for the second sock. Shown here with a Garter Cuff and Crenellated (Picot) Bind-Off.

Yarn:
Fingering weight sock yarn, 50 g = approximately 160-212 m/175-230 yds. Approximately 12-15 wraps per inch.
A plain pair of ankle length socks in the smaller sizes will require 100 g. For very long feet, larger ankle sizes or extended sock legs, allow extra yarn if using one of the shorter yardage yarns.

Needles:
A set of five, 2-2.75 mm (US # 0-2) double-pointed needles, 6-8" in length. An extra set of finer dpns is helpful for picking up the heel stitches.

Gauge:
For a sock to wear well, it is important to knit a dense fabric. Choose abnormally small needles for the size of the yarn and work a small stocking stitch swatch to ensure you are achieving a dense fabric. There is no need to measure this swatch.

Size:
Adult, adjustable. See directions. *(Trust me!)*

Garter Stitch Toe Square

Two cast on options are given, 12 or 15 {4} stitches. Use the smaller figure for smaller ankle measurements (under 9") or the thicker sock yarns (giving gauges of less than 7 stitches per inch), and the larger toe square for larger ankles or thinner yarns.

There is considerable latitude to adjust the fit and sizing, regardless of the initial toe chosen.

Level: Intermediate

With contrasting WY, provisionally or regularly, cast on 12 (15) {4} stitches. Cut off WY.

With Main sock yarn,

Row 1: K12 (15) {4}.

To facilitate easy and neat picking up of the stitches around the sock toe, use two short pieces of brightly contrasting WY (one for each edge) to catch the working yarn as it changes direction from row to row. To avoid confusion use a different colour of WY than that used for the cast on edge.

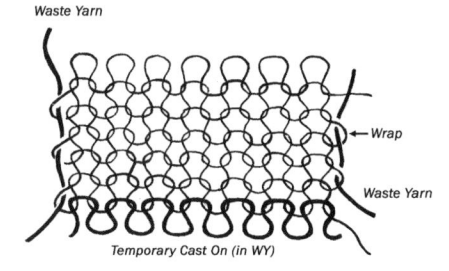

Diagram 5.

Row 2: W, k12 (15) {4}.

Repeat Row 2 until there are 12 (15) {4} wraps of the Main yarn around the WY at both sides of the square, 25 (31) {9} rows in total.

On completion of Row 25 (31) {9}, do not turn the work. With a new needle for each side, knit into each of the 12 (15) {4} Main yarn wraps (so as not to twist them) down the side of the square adjacent to the

working yarn. Remove the contrasting cast on edge (carefully cut it out, if necessary) and catch the resulting 11 (14) {3} stitches on a spare dpn; with the attached yarn knit across these stitches; knit up 12 (15) {4} more from the wraps up the remaining side. This will leave you with four needles in the work, three of which have 12 (15) {4} stitches, the other 11 (14) {3}.

Total 47 (59) {15} stitches. Remove the waste yarns.

Place beginning/end marker. *See Tip #10, page 8.*

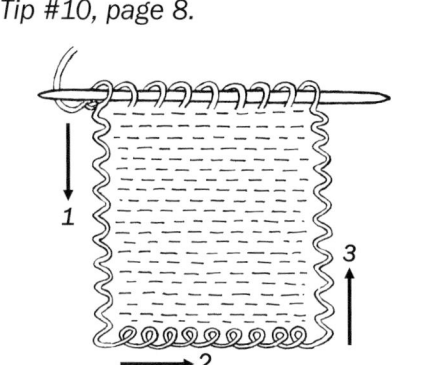

Diagram 6 illustrates the complete Toe Square and sequence in which to knit up the new stitches.

Round 1: Knit, making a single RSI in the middle of the 11 (14) {3} stitch side.

Total 48 (60) {16} stitches.

Knit 4 {2} rounds.

Begin making increases as given below. **Cease** increases as soon as the width of the sock fits the foot for which it is intended. Only you can determine this: slip the sock off the needles onto a thread of yarn to test the fit; err on the side of keeping the sock snug. For absentee feet, use a measurement of the foot circumference taken just before the toes begin to taper. Continue to increase until the fabric on the needles measures ½" less than the foot measurement. From this point omit the remaining increase rounds and continue knitting without further increases.

While working the increase section, either keep the stitches as set on the needles or mark the quarter round positions with additional markers of a different colour to the beginning/end marker and use the markers to reference the increase positions. The exact positioning is not critical. The increases are simply scattered fairly evenly around the sock. To personalize the toe shaping, adjust the number of knit rounds between the increase rounds; fewer plain rounds for a faster increase, more plain rounds for a slower increase.

Round 6 {4}: (K3, RSI, knit to end of needle) 4 times.   52 (64) {20} sts.
Knit 3 {1} rounds.

Crenellated Sock with Picot-Edged Stocking Stitch Facing, Turkish Heel and Bosnian Toe.

Round 10 {6}: (K12 {1}, RSI, knit to end of needle) 4 times.
56 (68) {24} sts.
{Stop increases here. Continue from Foot.}
Knit 4 rounds.

Round 15: (K6, RSI, knit to end of needle) 4 times.   60 (72) sts.
Don't forget to cease increases as soon as the sock fits!
Knit 5 rounds.

Round 21: (K10, RSI, knit to end of needle) 4 times.   64 (76) sts.
Knit 6 rounds.

Round 28: (K8, RSI, knit to end of needle) 4 times.   68 (80) sts.

Knit 6 rounds.

Round 35: (K1, RSI, knit to end of needle) 4 times.   72 (84) sts.

Knit 6 rounds.

Round 42: (K15, RSI, knit to end of needle) 4 times.   76 (88) sts.

If a larger foot size is needed, continue to increase in this scattered manner every seventh round until the sock foot is wide enough.

From this point, sock directions will be given according to the number of stitches in your round: 52 (56, **60**, 64, **68**, 72, **76**, 80, **84**, 88) {24} sts. *Highlight the figures relating to your sock size.*

Foot

Once the sock is wide enough for the foot, make no further increases. Knit in the round until the sock foot is 1¾ (1¾, 1¾, 2, **2**, 2, **2**, 2¼, **2¼**, 2¼) {½}" short of the heel-to-toe measurement. *This may be determined by comparative measurements of foot and sock or by slipping the sock stitches onto a length of yarn and trying on the sock.* Now determine how you wish the toe to lie, as a triangle or a rectangle. Knit around to the newly determined mid-point of the Instep stitches on the upper side of the sock.

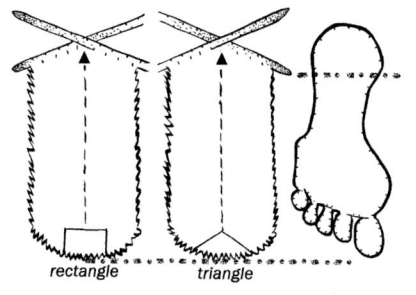

Diagram 7 illustrates the re-alignment of the foot tube for triangular or rectangular toes.

Heel Placement and Leg

K10 (11, **12**, 13, **14**, 14, **15**, 16, **17**, 18) {5} stitches, allow working yarn to dangle — do not disconnect. With a length of WY, knit the next 32 (34, **36**, 38, **40**, 44, **46**, 48, **50**, 52) {14} stitches. Cut off the WY, leaving a tail. Slip the WY stitches back onto the LHN (as necessary), and resume knitting with the working yarn; knit across the top of the WY stitches. See *Diagram 8, page 34.* Having worked across half of the WY stitches, place a centre-back marker.

To create the leg, continue in stocking stitch for as many inches above the heel WY as you wish.

At the marker position, change to the chosen cuff pattern.

Cuff Options 1-5:

1 - Garter Cuff with Smooth Bind-Off

For an emphatic start to the garter stitch cuff, make the first purl round on the second round of a new colour. This will give a solid coloured garter ridge.

Round 1: Purl one round.

Round 2: Knit one round.

Repeat these two rounds until the cuff is of sufficient length. End with a Round 1.

For a smooth edge, bind off very loosely *knitwise*; try using either the Modified Conventional Bind-Off *(see page 120)* or a larger needle in the right hand. It is always a challenge to make a neat bound-off edge with sufficient elasticity to admit the ankle. Try the sock on before cutting off the yarn.

2 - Garter Cuff with Crenellated (Picot) Bind-Off

Work as above until completion of the final Round 1. {*See Modified Crenellated Edge, page 62.*}

Bind off 3 stitches as usual, return the remaining stitch on the RHN purlwise to the LHN. Into this slipped stitch ✱✱ insert the RHN as if to knit, knit and draw a new loop of yarn through this stitch and place the resulting loop onto the LHN✱✱✱.

One extra stitch has now been created. Into the outermost stitch on the LHN, repeat from ✱✱ to ✱✱✱, three times more until four new stitches are created in total. Bind off five stitches as usual.

Repeat around the edge until all the sock stitches have been bound off.

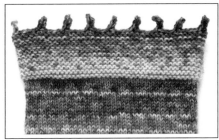

Crenellated Sock with Garter Cuff and Crenellated (Picot) Bind-Off.

3 - Rib Cuff Single Layer 2 x 2 Rib with Expanded Bind-Off

Begin a (k2, p2) rib and continue for as long as desired. To avoid any possibility of a tight upper edge, either change the needles to a larger size a few rounds before the top or increase on the final round as follows: (K1, m1, k1, p2) repeat to end.

Bind off very gently in 3 x 2 rib.

An extra long ribbing may also be folded or slouched down.

4 - Double-Layer Rib Cuff

If you desire a double-layer cuff, rib, as above, to the desired height.

Create a turning round by purling one or more rounds (up to 3 rounds) and continue in rib beginning with (p2, k2). *The new rib is the reverse of the old to allow the corrugations to stack neatly within each other.* When the facing is equal in length, it may be gently bound off and sewn inside the sock or grafted directly in place without binding off.

5 - Picot-Edged Stocking Stitch Facing

Continue in stocking stitch as set until the desired sock height is reached. If you are taking the sock well up the leg, you may incrementally increase the needle size as you go.

Once the desired height is reached, work one picot round; (O, k2t) repeat, before resuming stocking stitch. After the first plain knit round, either decrease the needle size or reduce the number of stitches by 10%. Continue knitting on the facing until it is of the desired length to control the sock top, at least ¾ {¼}". Bind off extremely loosely or invert the sock and graft the stitches, one by one, to the inside of the sock leg.

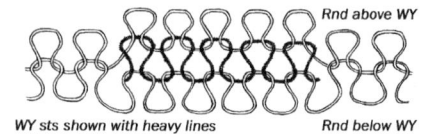

WY sts shown with heavy lines   Rnd below WY

Diagram 8 illustrates the WY set in place for the Turkish Heel.

Turkish Heel

With the toe pointing downwards, take a fine dpn and thread it under the RHS of each of the 32 (34, **36**, 38, **40**, 44, **46**, 48, **50**, 52) {14} Main yarn stitches immediately below the WY stitches. Place the first half of the stitches on one dpn and the remainder on another.

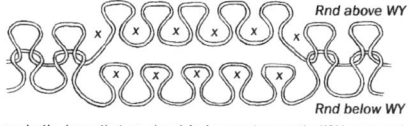

x marks the loops that may be picked up as sts once the WY is removed

Diagram 9 illustrates the potential stitches released when the WY is removed.

Turn the sock, toe up, and slide the third and fourth needles, in turn, under the RHS of each of the Main yarn "stitches" on the opposite side of the WY, 32 (34, **36**, 38, **40**, 44, **46**, 48, **50**, 52) {14} stitches, plus one more stitch at the end. Total 33 (35, **37**, 39, **41**, 45, **47**, 49, **51**, 53) {15} stitches on these needles. Cut or pull out the WY.

Round 1: With regular size dpns, RS facing, and beginning at the side of the sock, knit across the 32 (34, **36**, 38, **40**, 44, **46**, 48, **50**, 52) {14} Sole stitches; begin Needle #3 with k2t, knit to end of round, total 64 (68, **72**, 76, **80**, 88, **92**, 96, **100**, 104) {28} stitches. Divide the stitches a quarter per needle.

Rounds 2 & 3 {2}: Knit. *Don't panic, there will be significant gaps at the corners at this point.*

Keep stitches on the needles as given until the decreases are established.

Round 4 {3}: (Decrease Round) Needle #1, K1, ssk, knit to last 3 stitches of Needle #2, k2t, k1, Needle #3, k1, ssk, knit to last 3 stitches of Needle #4, end k2t, k1.

From this point, make decrease rounds every third round, twice {zero times}, and then every alternate round.

Try on the sock regularly. Once the heel is nearly deep enough, work the decrease round every round until 1-1½" width of stitches remains, approximately 20-30 stitches in the round, dependent on yarn and sock size.

{Decrease on alternate rounds until 12 stitches remain.}

This heel is very adaptable. For extra depth, insert extra plain rounds, thus slowing the rate of decrease or vice versa.

Finishing

Graft the heel stitches together, neaten the gaps at either side of the heel and darn in all the ends. *See page 98 for sock finishing techniques.*

Variations

The heel may be worked in another yarn altogether if you are short of the original yarn.

If you wish to create extra strength and thickness in the heel, work single stitches with two yarns alternately, use a contrast colour or another piece of matching yarn for your second strand or weave in an extra yarn at the back of the work. Toe-up socks can easily be extended into knee socks *(see page 96)*.

Marietta Rib Socks

A ribbed sock with attitude. Offered in a wide range of sizes, with a choice of optional frilled tops for a flamboyant and elastic upper edge. The foot has a ribbed upper for a snug fit. Shown here with a Scalloped Turn-Over Top.

Yarn:
Fingering weight sock yarn, 50 g = approximately 160-212 m/175-230 yds. Approximately 12-15 wraps per inch.
A pair of ankle length socks in the smaller sizes will require 100 g. For very long feet, larger ankle sizes or extended sock legs, allow extra yarn if using one of the shorter yardage yarns.

Gauge:
For a sock to wear well, it is important to knit a dense fabric. Take your chosen yarn and work a stocking stitch swatch 30 stitches wide on fine needles. Work on the finest size needles that you find comfortable. Once you have settled on a suitable gauge, measure the number of stitches per inch you are achieving; do not round off any fractions of stitches.

Needles:
A set of five, 2-2.75 mm (US # 0-2) double-pointed needles, 6-8" in length.
A 40 cm (16") circular needle in gauge size is helpful for the first round(s) of Scalloped or Ruffled edges.

Size:
Measure ankle circumference (just above the joint), in inches.

How Many Stitches Do I Need?
Multiply your stitches/inch gauge figure by the ankle measurement in inches. Example at 7.25 sts per inch with a 9½" ankle = 68.87 sts. Round the figure UP to the nearest multiple of 4 (in this case 72 sts).
Pick your size from 64 (68, **72**, 76, **80**, 84, **88**) stitches.

Sock Cast On
Select your chosen sock start method: Scalloped, Ruffled or Plain.

The Scalloped and Ruffled edges require a lot of stitches. The cast on will be very long and initially appear far too large for a sock. It is easiest to begin on a 40 cm/16" circular needle.

Remember that you will be looking at the underside of these edges as you work them; they later fold over

Level: Beginner

to reveal their true beauty. (See Colour in Cast-On Edges, page 91.)

Scalloped Turn-Over Top

Using Long Tail method *(see page 105)* and circular gauge-sized needle {dpns}, cast on 160 (170, **180**, 190, **200**, 210, **220**) {60} stitches.

Round 1: Purl one round.

With a set of 5 needles (for easy stitch handling use well-pointed needles) in gauge-size, work scallop round below.

Scallop Round: ✻✻ P2, slip the second stitch back to the LHN purlwise, lift the following **seven** stitches in turn over the slipped stitch and off the needle (a seven stitch decrease), 0, p1 *(the slipped stitch with the seven others on it)*, p1.

There should now be four stitches (or a multiple thereof) on the RHN at the completion of each repeat.

Repeat from ✻✻ 16 (17, **18**, 19, **20**, 21, **22**) {6} times in total.

64 (68, **72**, 76, **80**, 84, **88**) {24} stitches remain.

Work approximately a quarter of the number of scallops onto each dpn, in turn, until all four working needles are used.

Round 3: Purl one round.
Round 4: (K1, p1) repeat.
Round 5: (P1, k1) repeat.

Round 6: (K1, p1) repeat.
Rounds 7-12 {7-9}: Knit.

Continue as given below for ALL Sock Styles.

Ruffled Turn-Over Top

Using Long Tail method *(see page 105)* and circular gauge-sized needle {dpns}, cast on 154 (161, **168**, 182, **189**, 196, **203**) {56} sts.

Rounds 1-4: (K1, p5, k1) repeat.

Round 5: Decrease Round - (k1, p1, PWDD, p1, k1) repeat. 110 (115, **120**, 130, **135**, 140, **145**) {40} sts.

Rounds 6-8: (K1, p3, k1) repeat.

Round 9: Second Decrease Round - (k1, PWDD, k1) repeat.
66 (69, **72**, 78, **81**, 84, **87**) {24} sts.

PWDD Purlwise double decrease:
With yarn in purl position, slip knitwise two stitches one at a time to the RHN, insert tip of LHN into the inner, then the outer, of the two slipped stitches and return them to the LHN, p3t.

*The **knitwise** slipping alters the order of the stitches so that when the decrease (p3t) is made, it lies centrally about the middle stitch.*

Rounds 10-14 {10, 11}: Knit.

Round 15 {12}: Knit, making 2 (1, **0**, 2, **1**, 0, **0**✻) {0} evenly spaced decreases. ✻Largest size ONLY - increase 1 stitch.

64 (68, **72**, 76, **80**, 84, **88**) {24} sts.

Continue as given below for ALL Sock Styles.

Plain Cast-On Socks

Using Long Tail method *(see page 105)*, cast on 64 (68, **72**, 76, **80**, 84, **88**) {24} stitches. Pay special attention to spacing the stitches a little further apart than usual on the needle as you create them, to ensure an elastic edge. *See Tip #8, page 8.*

Continue as given below for ALL Sock Styles.

ALL Sock Styles

Rib Round: (K1, p2, k1) repeat.

Work rounds of 2 x 2 rib as set, until the sock leg is long enough, approximately 3-5" {1-2"} from the turn or plain cast on edge. Place a marker to mark the beginning/end point of the rounds. *See Tips #6 and #10.*

Make Heel Flap

Rib 16 (16, **20**, 20, **20**, 20, **24**) {8} stitches past beginning/end point. Turn.

(Note that the centre back position of sizes #3, #4 and #7 {and mini} is moved across by 2 stitches to keep the rib aligned.)

With WS facing: S1, (k2, p2) 7 (7, **8**, 8, **9**, 9, **10**) {2} times, end k2, p1. Turn.

These 32 (32, **36**, 36, **40**, 40, **44**) {12} stitches form the heel flap. Continue the heel flap on these stitches.

Slip the remaining 32 (36, **36**, 40, **40**, 44, **44**) {12} Instep stitches onto a holder.

Row 1: (RS) S1, [p1, wyib s1, k1, s1] 7 (7, **8**, 8, **9**, 9, **10**) {2} times, end p1, wyib s1, k1.

Row 2: (WS) S1, [k2, p2] 7 (7, **8**, 8, **9**, 9, **10**) {2} times, end k2, p1.

Repeat these last two rows 19 (20, **21**, 22, **23**, 24, **25**) {7} times in total, or until the heel flap is as long as it is wide. Fold the flap on a diagonal to check.

Turning the Heel

Working on your 32 (32, **36**, 36, **40**, 40, **44**) {12} heel flap stitches, begin the heel turning rows as given.

Row 1: (RS) S1, rib 22 (22, **24**, 24, **26**, 26, **28**) {6}, ssk, k1, turn. 6 (6, **8**, 8, **10**, 10, **12**) {2} stitches remain unworked on the LHN.

Row 2: (WS) S1, p15 {3}, p2t, p1, turn. 6 (6, **8**, 8, **10**, 10, **12**) {2} stitches remain unworked on the LHN.

Row 3: S1, k16 {4}, ssk, k1, turn.

Row 4: S1, p17 {5}, p2t, p1, turn. {Mini complete, do not turn. 8 Heel stitches remain.}

Row 5: S1, k18, ssk, k1, turn.

Row 6: S1, p19, p2t, p1, turn.

Row 7: S1, k20, ssk, k1, turn.

Row 8: S1, p21, p2t, p1, turn.

Sizes #1 and #2 only, heel complete, do not turn. 24 Heel stitches remain.

Row 9: S1, k22, ssk, k1, turn.

Row 10: S1, p23, p2t, p1, turn.

Sizes #3 and #4 only, heel complete, do not turn. 26 Heel stitches remain.

Row 11: S1, k24, ssk, k1, turn.

Row 12: S1, p25, p2t, p1, turn.

Sizes #5 and #6 only, heel complete, do not turn. 28 Heel stitches remain.

Row 13: S1, k26, ssk, k1, turn.

Row 14: S1, p27, p2t, p1. Size #7, 30 Heel stitches remain.

All Sizes: S1, knit across remaining 23 (23, **25**, 25, **27**, 27, **29**) {7} Heel stitches.

Knit Up Round - Replace the Instep stitches onto a dpn.

Needle #1: Knit up 19 (20, **21**, 22, **23**, 24, **25**) {7} stitches into the back of the outer side of each of the slipped edge stitches of the heel flap (or one stitch per edge stitch if you have a different number of Heel Flap rows).

Work the first 4 stitches from the Instep in pattern, k1, p2, k1 onto this needle also.

23 (24, **25**, 26, **27**, 28, **29**) {11} sts.

Needle #2: Work in rib, to last 4 Instep stitches.

24 (28, **28**, 32, **32**, 36, **36**) {4} sts.

Needle #3: Rib final 4 Instep stitches. Knit up 19 (20, **21**, 22, **23**, 24, **25**) {7} stitches along side of heel flap as before.

23 (24, **25**, 26, **27**, 28, **29**) {11} sts.

Needle #4: Knit across the 24 (24, **26**, 26, **28**, 28, **30**) {8} Heel stitches.

Instep Decrease Round

Needle #1: Knit to last 5 stitches, end k2t, p2, k1.

Needle #2: Work in rib as set across needle.

Needle #3: K1, p2, ssk, knit to end.

Needle #4: Knit to end.

Continue to work decrease rounds every round until 64 (68, **72**, 76, **80**, 84, **88**) {24} stitches remain.

Work as set until 1½ {½}" short of desired foot length.

Stocking Stitch Common Wedge Toe

Knit one round (cease rib pattern across the Instep), finish at the mid-point of the sole. Place a marker at this point. Dividing the stitchs into a quarter per needle from this marked position. 16 (17, **18**, 19, **20**, 21, **22**) {6} stitches per needle.

The photograph above shows the Marietta Rib Sock with an extended leg and Scalloped Turn-Over Top.

Count carefully as the Sole and Instep may have differing numbers of stitches. See Diagram 2, page 18. Now work from Toe Decrease Round page 19.

The Marietta Rib Sock above has a Ruffled Turn-Over Top.

Finishing

Graft the toe stitches together, neaten the small gaps at either side of the Instep and darn in all the ends. *See page 98 for sock finishing techniques.*

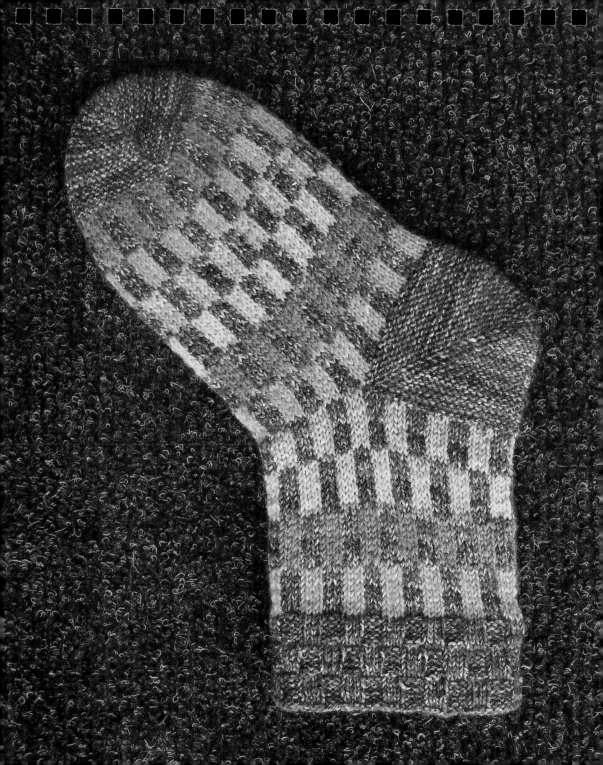

Chequerboard Socks

Spice up your self-striping sock yarns with this toe-up sock. Start with a single-yarn, Garter Stitch Short Row Toe worked on two needles, then knit in the round with a two-colour-per-round chequered pattern.

This pattern is designed to give a new look to a yarn that would usually give stripes when used singly. The use of garter stitch for the heel and toe, and two-colour-per-round patterning, make for a strong, cozy sock throughout. Shown here with a Textured Faced Chequerboard Cuff.

Yarn:
Fingering weight sock yarn (in two colours), 50 g = approximately 160-212 m/175-230 yds. Approximately 12 -15 wraps per inch.

Smaller sizes will require 50 g of each yarn. For long feet, larger ankle sizes or extended sock legs, or if using one of the shorter yardage yarns, allow extra Background yarn. See Yarn Colour Selection page 44.

Gauge:
For a sock to wear well, it is important to knit a dense fabric by using fine needles. On the smallest needles that you can stand, work a 32 stitch swatch in the 3 x 3 Chequerboard pattern as given below. Once you have settled on a suitable gauge, measure the number of stitches per inch you are achieving over the central portion of the swatch; do not round off any fractions of stitches.

Needles:
Two sets of five dpns, 6-8" in length: one in gauge size for the Chequerboard pattern (2.25-3 mm/US # 1-3), and a second set one size smaller (2-2.75 mm/US # 0-2) for the toe, heel and cuff.

Size:
Measure the ankle circumference (just above the joint), in inches.

How Many Stitches Do I Need?
Multiply your stitches/inch gauge figure by the ankle measurement in inches. Example at 7.5 sts per inch with a 9½" ankle = 71.25 sts. Round the figure up or down to the nearest multiple of 6 (in this case 72 sts).

Pick your size from 54 (60, **66**, 72, **78**, 84) sts. Armed with this figure, go to Garter Stitch Short Row Toe.

Level: Sock Goddess

Yarn Colour Selection

Two contrasting yarns are required: Background (B) in a solid colour, and Contrast (C). For maximum effect Yarn C should have long sections of colour with distinct colour change points. A subtly shaded yarn may also be used, or a second solid yarn, but each will give a different look. See Variations at the end of the pattern.

Chequerboard Pattern Swatch Details

A 3 x 3 pattern is used throughout the two-colour-per-round section. In order to prevent corrugations and excessive colour-show-through, yet also to keep the floats in the sock to a minimum, weave-in the secondary colour about the middle stitch of each colour block on alternate rounds only. Work the intervening rounds without any weaving of the yarns.

Swatch: (Worked flat) Onto a single dpn, cast on 32 stitches.

Row 1: (RS) With both yarns together k1, weave the yarn being carried behind the middle stitch of each group of stitches as you work (k3C, k3B), repeat to last stitch, end k1 with both yarns together. Do not turn the work around. Slide the work to the opposite end of the needle with RS facing you, bring both yarns gently across the back of the work ready to be used for Row 2.

Row 2: (RS) *Treat the first and last stitches as single stitches. The purpose of doubling is only to secure both yarns at the sides.* With both yarns together k1, without weaving (k3C, k3B) repeat to last stitch, end k1 with both yarns together.

Repeat Swatch Rows 1 and 2 until you have a swatch at least 1½" long.

Wash, block and take measurements across the central area.

Garter Stitch Short Row Toe:

To fit sock sizes 54 (60, **66**, 72, **78**, 84) {24} stitches.

With contrasting WY and needles one size smaller than those used for the gauge in the Chequerboard pattern, PCCO 27 (30, **33**, 36, **39**, 42) {12} stitches onto a single dpn. Cut off WY. *See page 110.*

Rows 1 and 2: With Yarn B, knit. *RS toe rows are ODD numbered.*

Row 3: K26 (29, **32**, 35, **38**, 41) {11}, s1.

Row 4: Slip the first stitch across to the new RHN, with the working yarn around the first slipped stitch, k25 (28, **31**, 34, **37**, 40) {10}, s1.

Row 5: Slip the first stitch across to the new RHN, with the working yarn around the first stitch, k24 (27, **30**, 33, **36**, 39) {9}, SWR.

Note: the newly wrapped stitch is replaced before turning from this row onwards, until the final RS and WS toe rows.

Row 6: **Knit to one stitch before last wrapped stitch, [23 (26, **29**, 32, **35**, 38) {8} stitches], SWR.**

At this point and on completion of every WS row (even numbered), there should be an equal number of wrapped stitches on either side of the toe.

Repeat from ** to ** working one less knit stitch on each successive row, until the WS row is k7 (8, **9**, 10, **11**, 12) {4}, SWR ; giving 10 (11, **12**, 13, **14**, 15) {4} wrapped stitches on either side.

Now commence the gradually increasing rows. *The last stitch that you knit before the SWR will have a wrap around it (or wraps on subsequent rows); ignore the wrap(s) other than as a reference, knit the stitch as usual. Do not knit the "wrap" together with the stitch as you would for wrapped stitches in a stocking stitch fabric.*

K8 (9, **10**, 11, **12**, 13) {5}, SWR.
K9 (10, **11**, 12, **13**, 14) {6}, SWR.

Continue until only the last and first stitches are unwrapped.

The final RS row will be: k24 (27, **30**, 33, **36**, 39) {9}, slip the last stitch, unworked, from the left needle to the right, turn.

The final WS row will be: Slip the previously slipped stitch across to the new RHN, with the working yarn around it, k25 (28, **31**, 34, **37**, 40) {10}, slip the last stitch, unworked, from the left needle to the right, turn.

Completing the Toe and Establishing Knitting in the Round

With RS facing, slip the first stitch across to the new RHN, with the working yarn around it, k26 (27, **32**, 35, **38**, 41) {11}.

Work half of the stitches onto one dpn, the second half onto another.

Unravel the PCCO edge, stitch by stitch, catch the resulting 26 (29, **32**, 35, **38**, 41) {11} "stitches" on an empty dpn. *There should be one less "stitch" than you originally cast on, as you are actually picking up the loops between the original stitches; the final partial loop of Yarn B (after the slip knot) should be ignored.*

Share the new stitches between two dpns.

Resume work with Yarn B, knitting across the 26 (29, **32**, 35, **38**, 41) {11} new "stitches".

With the RHN knit up one new stitch from the side edge of the toe fabric, between the needles, to bring the total stitch count up to 54 (60, **66**, 72, **78**, 84) {24}; continuing in the round, **purl** across the 27 (30, **33**, 36, **39**, 42) {12} stitches of the toe. Place a marker at the beginning/ end point of the round.

Chequerboard Pattern Foot

First find an appropriate position in the colour sequence of the space-dyed yarn from which to begin. Unwind a length of Yarn C and locate the first convenient colour change. Cut off any excess yarn.

Beginning at the side of the toe, with your **larger** needles (gauge size) begin the Chequerboard pattern as follows:

Round 1: Weaving in as given for the swatch, (K3C, k3B) repeat to end of round.

Round 2: Floating yarns across each colour in turn (without weaving), (K3C, k3B) repeat to end of round.

Making the Colours Form a Chequerboard Pattern

Repeat Rounds 1 and 2 as given until a change in the Yarn C colour is reached, complete a final group of three Yarn C stitches. Break the established (k3C, k3B) pattern by working 6 consecutive stitches in Yarn B. Weave Yarn C in behind these 6 stitches to prevent a long float, regardless of whether it is a weaving round or not. Then resume (k3C, k3B) pattern.

From This Point On ...

Continue to alternate the weaving and non-weaving rounds, switching at the beginning/end marker position.

Change the Chequerboard pattern, as above, whenever Yarn C dictates.

Continue as set until the foot is 1½ (1½, **1¾**, 1¾, **2**, 2) {½}" short of the desired foot length.

Stop 3 {1} stitches before marker. The next 33 (36, **39**, 42, **45**, 48) {14} stitches will become the heel.

Garter Stitch Short Row Heel

Use a new piece of Yarn B for the heel. This will be referred to as the Heel yarn.

Do not cut off the already attached yarns B and C.

If you have only one ball of B, use the opposite end to the one you are working from for the duration of the heel. The separate heel yarn will give the neatest possible heel corners. If you cannot abide this complication, or cannot easily access the other end of your yarn, cut off Yarn B, leaving a couple of meters/yards attached, so that the join in Yarn B will occur further down the sock, a round or two beyond the heel.

Link the tail of the new Heel yarn around both of the former working yarns. As you knit the first stitches of the heel with the new Heel yarn, you may weave in the tail of the Heel yarn at the back of the work, to simultaneously prevent a future gap and to neaten the tail.

With your **smaller** needle and the new piece of Heel yarn B, knit the first 16 (17, **19**, 20, **22**, 23) {7} heel stitches onto an empty dpn. Then onto a second dpn knit the next 16 (18, **19**, 21, **22**, 24) {6} stitches, SWR. The wrapped and replaced stitch will be on the adjacent needle next to the Instep stitches. *This stitch has a "wrap" of the heel yarn around its base but remains in its original colour.*

Divide the remaining 21 (24, **27**, 30, **33**, 36) {10} stitches (the Instep) onto two dpns along with the one "wrapped" heel stitch. *See Diagram #4, page 25.*

Turn the work around WS facing. With an empty dpn (use a second dpn for the last half of the heel stitches), knit until only the first Heel stitch remains unworked, [k31 (34, **37**, 40, **43**, 46) {12}], SWR (onto the adjacent needle holding the Instep stitches).

Subsequent Right and Wrong Side Rows

Turn the work RS facing; with an empty dpn, knit until one Heel stitch remains unworked on the LHN [k30 (33, **36**, 39, **42**, 45) {11}], SWR.

Turn the work WS facing, knit until one heel stitch remains unworked on LHN [k29 (32, **35**, 38, **41**, 44) {10}], SWR.

As an aid to keeping on track, there should always be the same number of "wrapped" stitches on either side of the heel on the completion of each WS row. Remember that the first "wrapped" stitch on the LHS is in the Main yarn colour.

Repeat these two rows until the heel is deep enough for your foot, end with a WS row, approximately [k7 (8, **9**, 10, **9,** 10) {2}, SWR]. There should be an equal number of "wrapped" stitches on either side of the central 7 to 10 {2} stitches.

Suggested Stitch Distribution

Initially, when working the heel stitches on two dpns: on both RS and WS rows, knit two extra stitches onto the old needle before introducing the empty dpn. This staggers the junction of the work and helps to prevent distortion down the centre line of the heel.

When the number of working heel stitches is sufficiently reduced, work them onto a single dpn, and use the spare needle to hold the middle section of the Instep stitches. This greatly increases working comfort.

Heel Increase Section

RS Facing: Knit an equal number of stitches as in the previous row [k7 (8, **9**, 10, **9**, 10) {2}], knit 1 previously "wrapped" stitch from the next needle. Work this stitch as usual, leaving the "wrap" around the base of the stitch. Slip the next heel stitch from the Instep needle to the RHN, bring the yarn between the needles (making a wrap), and return the slipped stitch to the Instep needle. Turn.

WS Facing: Knit across all the stitches on the heel needles [k8 (9, **10**, 11, **10**, 11) {3}], knit 1 previously "wrapped" stitch from the next needle (work the stitch as usual), slip the next heel stitch from the Instep needle to the RHN, bring the yarn between the needles (making a wrap) and return it to the Instep needle. Turn.

RS Facing: Knit across all the stitches on the heel needles [k9 (10, **11**, 12, **11**, 12) {4}], knit 1 previously "wrapped" stitch from the next needle (work the stitch as usual), slip next heel stitch from the Instep needle to the RHN, bring the yarn between the needles (making a wrap) and return it to the Instep needle. Turn.

Repeat these two rows, increasing by one the number of stitches worked on each successive row, until the last heel stitch has received its second wrap. End with a WS row [k30 (33, **36**, 39, **42**, 45) {11} plus 1 previously "wrapped" stitch], wrap the heel yarn around the first heel stitch, but do not return the wrapped stitch to the LHN. Turn. Cut off the heel yarn, leaving a tail.

Resuming with your **larger** needles (gauge size) and the Main working yarns B and C, tighten up any slack that has crept into the last stitch worked in the Main yarn. Resume the Chequerboard pattern, as set, across the Heel stitches. The tail of the Heel yarn may be woven in as you go. Maintain the marker and work as previously given.

Work until the leg length is approximately 1½" {½"} short of the desired overall length. Finish the round at the marker, or at the centre back, or at a convenient point in the colour sequence of yarn C.

Cut off Yarn C. Place a marker at the commencement of the Cuff if necessary.

Textured Chequerboard Cuff

With Yarn B, and changing to **smaller** dpns:

Round 1: Knit.

Rounds 2-6 {2, 3}: (K3, p3) repeat.

Round 7 {4}: Knit.

Rounds 8-12 {5, 6}: (P3, k3) repeat. Repeat Rounds 1-6 {1-3}.

Rounds 19-20 {10, 11}: Purl. *These are the turning rounds; extra purl rounds may be added for a softer rolled edge.*

Rounds 21-38 {12-16}: (K3, p3) repeat.

Check that the length of the inner facing matches that of the outer. Turn the sock inside out on the needles to test; add or subtract rounds as necessary.

Finish the cuff by binding off, exceedingly loosely. (It will be out of sight inside the sock — get sloppy!) Alternatively, cut off Yarn B with enough tail length to permit grafting the final round of stitches back to the stitches of the last round of the two-colour knitting. Grafting in this situation doesn't have to be impeccable as long as all the live stitches are secured and the grafting is loose enough to give a top with equal elasticity to the rest of the sock.

Finishing

If you cast off the cuff, catch-stitch the facing gently around the sock top, checking the elasticity of the bind off and stitching.

Reinforce the stitches on either side of the heel and darn in all the ends. *See page 98 for sock finishing techniques.*

Variations

The sock can be worked with any style of contrasting yarn, plain, speckled, or shaded; however, you will have to dictate when the chequers change. Chequers may be a uniform number of rounds or alternating long and short unequal rectangles.

The width of the columns of stitches (here 3 stitches wide) may be adjusted, either in a repeating sequence around the sock or simply to taste.

Bands of single colour stripes can be interspersed with chequered sections. (Use smaller needles for the single-yarn sections!)

■ ■ ■ ■ ■ ■ ■ ■ ■ ■ ■ ■ ■ ■ ■ ■ ■ ■ ■ ■

Mermaid Socks

A dramatic single-yarn sock, featuring an Estonian Fishtail stitch pattern. Two cuff options are given — a simple Wavy Cuff (no grafting required) or a more elaborate Sideways Garter Stitch Cuff (no swatching required).

Yarn:

Fingering weight sock yarn, 50 g = approximately 160-212m/175-230 yds. Approximately 12-15 wraps per inch. For maximum impact, choose a self-striping yarn with strong contrasts and abrupt colour changes (avoid speckled yarns).

A plain pair of ankle length socks in the smaller sizes will require 100 g. For very long feet, larger ankle sizes or extended sock legs, allow extra yarn if using one of the shorter yardage yarns.

Needles:

Two sets of 5 dpns: for Sideways Garter Stitch Cuff, Heel and Toe, choose the smallest size you can comfortably use, and a set one or two sizes larger for the Fishtail (diagonal) section of the sock.

Suggested smaller needle sizes 2-2.75 mm (US # 0-2½) with larger needle sizes 2.25-3.0 mm (US # 1-3).

Swatching:

Sideways Garter Stitch Cuff (pictured above). There is no need to swatch for this cuff style. The number of stitches required for your size of sock will be determined by the number of rows in the Cuff. The cuff is worked (using the **smaller** needle size) until it will fit the ankle measurement of the future wearer.

Swatching:

Wavy Cuff (see page 59). Work a stocking stitch swatch 30 stitches wide on the finest size needles that you find comfortable. Measure the number of stitches per inch you are achieving; do not round off any fractions of stitches. Multiply the gauge figure (sts/in) by the required ankle circumference (measured above the ankle joint in inches). The result will be the approximate number of stitches required for your sock. Round this figure up to the nearest one of the following figures 54 (60, **66**, 72, **78**, 84, **90**) sts.

Level: Sock Goddess

Sideways Garter Stitch Cuff

The sideways sock top itself acts as a gauge swatch and thus the number of rows in the length of the cuff determines the number of stitches needed for your sock. *The height of one garter stitch ridge, formed by two knit rows, is equal to the width of one stitch of stocking stitch when worked with the same yarn and needles.*

For the sideways cuff, use of the WY cast-on and bind-off, coupled with precise grafting, will give a seamless cuff. If you prefer, the option for conventional Cast-on/off is given on page 53.

WY Cast-On For Grafted Cuff

Onto **smaller** needles, with a contrasting colour, similar weight WY, cast on 15 {5} stitches. Work 6 rows of stocking stitch beginning with a knit row. Cut off WY and temporarily knot on Main yarn.

Row 1: (RS) In Main yarn, k15 {5}.

Row 2: (WS) In Main yarn, k14 {4}, p1.

Repeat these 2 rows until the cuff fits around the future wearer's ankle or is the same length as the ankle circumference, measured above the ankle joint. {Repeat these two rows 22 times more.}

WY Bind Off For Grafted Cuff

End with Row 1. Leaving sufficient yarn to later graft the last row, cut off the Main yarn.

Tie on a new length of WY with a temporary knot.

Work Row 2 **in pattern** in WY.

In WY work a further 5 rows in stocking stitch (beginning with a knit row).

Bind off the WY or slip the live stitches onto a thread.

Grafting the Cuff

Untie the temporary knots, thread a fine blunt needle onto the length of Main yarn and fold the Cuff into a circle, with RS outermost.

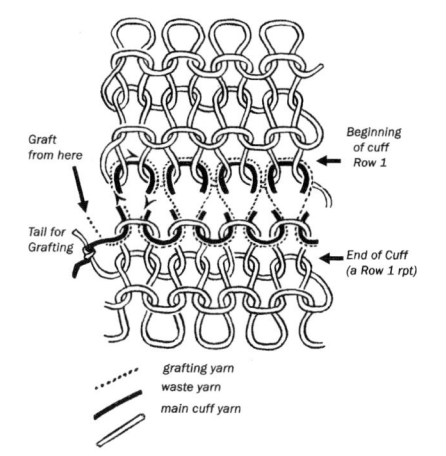

Diagram 10 illustrates the grafting of the cuff, right side facing, with the WY flaps tucked inside.

Tuck the WY flaps inside and hold them together so that you can see the stitches to be grafted. Using the tail of the Main yarn, graft the Main yarn stitches together by exactly following the path of the WY as it intersects with the Main yarn on either side.

When you are happy with the graft, remove both WY flaps. Leave the tails of the Main yarn to be neatened later. See Knit-Up Round below.

Conventional Cast-On/Off Method

Onto a **smaller** needle, with Main yarn, cast on 15 {5} stitches. Work from Row 1 as given above, bind off after final Row 2.

Seam the cast on and bound off edges to the inside of the work, leave the tails to neaten later.

Knit-Up Round (Sideways Cuff only)

Beginning at the centre back of the cuff, near to the seam line, or approximately 1 cm/½" to the left of the graft position, with Main yarn and one stitch from the lower edge of the cuff, knit up 1 stitch per garter ridge (2 rows) onto a set of dpns. Divide the stitches as equally as you can between the needles, preferably with a multiple of 6 stitches on each needle.

Count your stitches. The number of stitches will usually vary between 52-90 {24} stitches, according to the size of the ankle. Place the end-of-round marker.

Over the next few rounds, the number of stitches will need to be modified to the nearest multiple of 6 stitches. 54 (60, **66**, 72, **78**, 84, **90**) {24}. If you need to add or subtract stitches, a ⌘ is shown to indicate inconspicuous positions to modify your stitch count. There are three such positions indicated; if you need to gain or lose only one stitch, then pick the middle ⌘ position and ignore the other two.

{(Two rounds purl, 2 rounds knit), twice. Go to Fishtail Pattern Leg.}

Although numbers of plain and purl rounds have been suggested, you may choose to let the colour changes in the yarn dictate the number of rounds you use or the position at which you change from knit to purl (or vice versa). To achieve a distinctly coloured reverse stocking stitch band, change to purl one round after the colour changes.

Rounds 1-4: Purl.
Round 5: Knit. ⌘
Rounds 6-7: Knit.
Round 8: Knit. ⌘
Rounds 9-12: Purl.
Round 13: Knit. ⌘
Rounds 14-15: Knit.

Work as given for Fishtail Pattern Leg from this point.

Wavy Cuff

If a less elaborate, softer sock top is required, work a swatch and choose the number of stitches as given on page 51.

Note: *The swatch is worked on the **smaller** needles but the sock is cast on and worked onto the **larger** size.*

Onto larger dpns, cast on the required multiple of six stitches. [54 (60, **66**, 72, **78**, 84, **90**) {24} sts]

Round 1: Knit.

Round 2: Purl.

Round 3: Work in Fishtail pattern, (k2, 0, k2, k2t) repeat to end of round.

Round 4: Purl.

Repeat Rounds 3 and 4, 3 times (or more if desired) {once}; from this point, work as given for Fishtail Pattern Leg, but continue on your **larger** needles.

Fishtail Pattern Leg

With a multiple of 6 stitches [54 (60, **66**, 72, **78**, 84, **90**)] {24} and **a set of dpns one or two sizes larger** than used for the sideways cuff, work every round: K2, 0, k2, k2t. Repeat.

If you place a beginning/end running yarn marker, it will gradually spiral around the sock, so don't use it as a reference for placing the heel or toe.

Continue in Fishtail pattern as set until the leg length of the sock (above the heel) is sufficient.

This stitch pattern was discovered by Nancy Bush. Other applications can be found in her book, *Folk Knitting in Estonia,* Interweave Press.

Positioning the Heel

By eye, determine the approximate centre back position of your sock; choose and mark with a coil-less pin the middle stitch of one of the three side-by-side knit stitches that form the right-sloping ridges. It should be the stitch to the left of the k2t.

Work in pattern until 17 (18, **18**, 22, **23**, 24, **28**) {6} stitches remain *before* the marked stitch. The next 35 (37, **39**, 45, **47**, 51, **57**) {14} stitches will become the Heel stitches. The remaining 19 (23, **27**, 27, **31**, 33, **33**) {10} stitches will form the Instep stitches.

Garter Stitch Short Row Heel

Use **smaller** size dpns throughout the heel.

Use **a new piece of yarn** for the heel, even if you do not wish the heel to contrast. **Do not cut off** the Main working yarn.

If you have only one ball of yarn, use the opposite end to the one you are working from for the duration of the heel. The new yarn will give the neatest possible heel corners.

Link the tail of the new yarn around the former working yarn. Then, as you knit the first stitches of the heel, the tail of the Heel yarn may be woven in at the back of the work to simultaneously prevent a future gap and neaten the tail.

With the **new piece of Heel yarn**, knit the first half of the Heel stitches [17 (18, **19**, 22, **23**, 25, **28**) {7} stitches] onto an empty dpn, and the following 17 (18, **19**, 22, **23**, 25, **28**) {6} stitches onto another dpn, s1, bring the yarn between the needles, return the slipped stitch to the adjacent needle (next to the Instep stitches). This stitch has a "wrap" of the Heel yarn around its base but remains in the Main colour.

Divide the remaining 19 (23, **27**, 27, **31**, 33, **33**) {10} Instep stitches onto two dpns. *See Diagram 4.*

Turn the work around, WS facing. With an empty smaller size dpn (use a second dpn for the last half of the Heel stitches), [k33 (35, **37**, 43, **45**, 49, **55**) {12}], s1, bring the yarn between the needles, return the

slipped stitch to the adjacent needle holding the Instep stitches.

Subsequent Right and Wrong Side Rows

Turn the work RS facing, knit until one heel stitch remains unworked on LHN [k32 (34, **36**, 42, **44**, 48, **54**) {11}], SWR.

At this point the wrapped and replaced stitches should ideally be slipped onto spare smaller needles rather than the larger Instep needles. Add the first and last previously wrapped stitches to these needles. Be careful that the needle with the two stitches doesn't fall out; it will become firmer as more stitches are added.

Turn the work WS facing, knit until one heel stitch remains unworked on LHN [k31 (33, **35**, 41, **43**, 47, **53**) {10}], SWR.

As an aid to keeping on track, there should always be the same number of "wrapped" stitches on either side of the heel on the completion of each WS row. Remember that the first "wrapped" stitch on the LHS is in the Main colour.

Repeat these two rows, ending with a WS row, approximately [k7 (7, **7**, 7, **9**, 9, **9**) {2}, SWR] or until the heel is deep enough for your foot. There should be an equal number of "wrapped" stitches on either side of the central 7 or 9 {2} stitches.

Suggested Stitch Distribution

Initially, when working the heel stitches on two dpns: On both RS and WS rows, knit two extra stitches onto the old needle before introducing the empty dpn. This staggers the junction of the work and helps to prevent distortion down the centre-line of the heel.

When the number of working heel stitches is sufficiently reduced, work them onto a single dpn, and use the spare needle to hold the middle section of the Instep stitches. This greatly increases working comfort.

Heel Increase Section

RS Facing: Knit an equal number of stitches as are in the previous row [k7 (7, **7**, 7, **9**, 9, **9**) {2}], knit 1 previously "wrapped" stitch from the next needle. *Work this stitch as usual, leaving the "wrap" around the base of the stitch (don't knit into the wrap)*, slip the next heel stitch from the Instep needle to the RHN, bring the yarn between the needles (making a wrap) and return it to the Instep needle. Turn.

WS Facing: Knit across all the stitches on the heel needles [k8 (8, **8**, 8, **10**, 10, **10**) {3}], knit 1 previously "wrapped" stitch from the next needle—work the stitch as usual, SWR. Turn.

RS Facing: Knit across all the stitches on the heel needles [k9 (9, **9**, 9, **11**, 11, **11**) {4}], knit 1 previously "wrapped" stitch from the next needle—work the stitch as usual, SWR. Turn.

Repeat these two rows, increasing by one the number of stitches worked on each successive row, until the last heel stitch has received its second wrap. End with a WS row [k32 (34, **36**, 42, **44**, 48, **54**) {11} plus 1 previously "wrapped" stitch], wrap the heel yarn around the first heel stitch, but do not return the wrapped stitch to the LHN. Turn. Cut off the heel yarn, leaving a tail.

Resuming with the Main working yarn and **larger** dpns, tighten up any slack that has crept into the last stitch worked in the Main yarn, and knit across to the last Heel stitches. *The tail of the Heel yarn may be woven in as you work across the first half of the heel stitches.*

Once all of the heel stitches have been knit (including the final one which was only wrapped), resume the pattern. The first repeat will be: k2 (1, **5**, 3, **2**, 5, **3**) {6}, 0, k2, k2t, followed by the regular (k2, 0, k2, k2t) for all sizes.

Work in pattern until the sock is approximately 1½ (1½, **1½**, 1¾, **1¾**, 2, **2**) {½}" short of the desired foot length.

Spiral Toe

This is a softly shaped toe which retains the pattern appearance to the last moment.

Stay alert with the pattern (check off the rounds and use a marker), as it can become confusing.

Near the side of the sock, place a beginning-of-round marker after the completion of a full repeat. {Work Mini Spiral Toe page 61.}

Round 1: (K2, O, k2, k2t, k4, k2t) 4 (5, **5**, 6, **6**, 7, **7**) times, end (k2, O, k2, k2t) 1 (0, **1,** 0, **1,** 0, **1**) times. 50 (55, **61**, 66, **72,** 77, **83**) stitches remain.

Round 2: (K2, O, k2, k2t, k2, O, k1, k2t) 4 (5, **5,** 6, **6,** 7, **7**) times, end (k2, O, k2, k2t) 1 (0, **1,** 0, **1,** 0, **1**) times. 50 (55, **61,** 66, **72,** 77, **83**) sts.

Repeat **Round 2:** 1 (1, **2,** 2, **2,** 3, **3**) times more.

Round 3: (K4, k2t, k2, O, k1, k2t) 4 (5, **5,** 6, **6,** 7, **7**) times, end (k4, k2t) 1 (0, **1,** 0, **1,** 0, **1**) times. 45 (50, **55,** 60, **65,** 70, **75**) stitches remain.

Round 4: (K2, O, k1, k2t) 9 (10, **11,** 12, **13,** 14, **15**) times. 45 (50, **55,** 60, **65,** 70, **75**) sts.

Repeat **Round 4:** 1 (1, **2,** 2, **2,** 3, **3**) times more.

Round 5: (K2, O, k1, k2t, k3, k2t) 4 (5, **5,** 6, **6,** 7, **7**) times, end (k2, O, k1, k2t) 1 (0, **1,** 0, **1,** 0, **1**) times. 41 (45, **50,** 54, **59,** 63, **68**) stitches remain.

Round 6: (K2, O, k1, k2t, k2, O, k2t) 4 (5, **5,** 6, **6,** 7, **7**) times, end (k2, O, k1, k2t) 1 (0, **1,** 0, **1,** 0, **1**) times. 41 (45, **50,** 54, **59,** 63, **68**) sts.

Repeat **Round 6:** 0 (0, **1,** 1, **1,** 2, **2**) times more.

Round 7: (K3, k2t, k2, O, k2t) 4 (5, **5,** 6, **6,** 7, **7**) times, end (k3, k2t) 1 (0, **1,** 0, **1,** 0, **1**) times. 36 (40, **44,** 48, **52,** 56, **60**) stitches remain.

Round 8: (K2, O, k2t) 9 (10, **11,** 12, **13,** 14, **15**) times. 36 (40, **44,** 48, **52,** 56, **60**) sts.

Repeat **Round 8:** 0 (0, **1,** 1, **1,** 2, **2**) times more.

Round 9: (K2t, O, k2t) 9 (10, **11,** 12, **13,** 14, **15**) times. 27 (30, **33,** 36, **39,** 42, **45**) stitches remain.

Round 10: (K1, O, k2t) 9 (10, **11,** 12, **13,** 14, **15**) times. 27 (30, **33,** 36, **39,** 42, **45**) stitches remain.

Repeat **Round 10:** 0 (0, **1,** 1, **1,** 1, **1**) times more.

Round 11: (K1, k2t) 9 (10, **11**, 12, **13**, 14, **15**) times.
18 (20, **22**, 24, **26**, 28, **30**) stitches remain.

Round 12: Knit.

Round 13: K2t 9 (10, **11**, 12, **13**, 14, **15**) times.
9 (10, **11**, 12, **13**, 14, **15**) stitches remain.

Round 14: Knit

Round 15: *Very small dpns may be used for this round, if available.*
K2t 4 (5, **5**, 6, **6**, 7, **7**) times, end k1 1 (0, **1**, 0, **1**, 0, **1**) times. 5 (5, **6**, 6, **7**, 7, **8**) stitches remain.

Cut off the Main yarn leaving a 6" tail. Using a fine, blunt needle, thread the tail through all of the remaining stitches, beginning with the first stitch. Tighten the loop and gather the stitches before threading the yarn through the stitches once more.

Finishing

Reinforce the stitches on either side of the heel and darn in all the ends. *See page 98 for sock finishing techniques.*

Variations

Alternative style toes may also be used. For example, the Common Wedge toe in Garter Stitch would make a pleasing match to the heel and cuff. Adjust the frequency of the decrease rounds to suit your toe shape. Work it entirely in knit for a stocking stitch toe.

Due to the spiralling nature of the stitches and the directional nature of these toes, it is necessary to line up this type of toe with the heel by eye.

If you should run short of yarn, the heel and toe may be made in contrasting colours.

Alternative Toe: Garter Stitch Common Wedge Toe

Beginning at the side of the foot (check the toe/heel alignment), using **smaller** needles, divide the stitches a quarter per needle. If you are working with 54, 66, 78, or 90 stitches, decrease by 2 stitches before you divide. Place markers at both sides of the sock. {See page 62.} From the marker, work four rounds of garter stitch [(knit one round, purl one round) twice]. Continue from Round 1, page 27.

Below: Mermaid Sock with Wavy Cuff and Garter Stitch Turkish Heel.

Miniature Sock Information

All of these socks may be worked in miniature. This is an excellent way of trying all of the various techniques while using only a small amount of yarn and time. Miniature socks make great ornaments and gifts, not to mention extraordinary earrings and necklaces!

Because of the size of these socks, regular space-dyed sock yarns will give much larger blocks of colour and not be representative of the appearance of a full-sized sock.

Some general and pattern-specific details are suggested to make the miniaturization easy and successful. Stitch numbers for 24 stitch miniature socks are enclosed in { } throughout each pattern.

General Miniaturization Hints

1. Use short, lightweight needles.
2. It may be more comfortable to occasionally use only 3 needles in the round.
3. For easier handling, use larger needles than would be ideal for a real sock (durability isn't an issue) and thicker yarn than regular, fingering weight sock yarn. However, if you wish your socks to be as petite as possible, use the finest yarn and needles you can find!
4. Miniaturization can mean any multiple of four stitches less than full size. The sample socks have 24 stitches. (Fewer than 24 stitches and the sock begins to lose its proportion). For larger stitch number miniature socks, follow proportions and suggestions for Fit and Adjustments to alter the designs page 93.
5. Graft the toes with at least 12 stitches remaining. Fewer stitches make this very challenging. *Cheating is also quite permissible!* Slip the remaining toe stitches onto a thread of yarn. Cut off the Main yarn with 10" attached. Invert the sock (use a crochet-hook if necessary) and draw through the yarn tail, replace the instep and sole stitches on separate dpns and use the Main yarn tail to make a Three-Needle Bind-Off, *see page 119.*

Miniature Spiral Toe: *Used in Mermaid Socks*
Round 1: (K4, k2t) 4 times.
20 stitches remain.
Round 2: (K2, O, k1, k2t) 4 times.

Round 3: (K3, k2t) 4 times. 16 stitches remain.

Round 4: (K2, O, k2t) 4 times.

Round 5: (k2t, O, k2t) 4 times. 12 stitches remain.

Round 6: (k1, k2t) 4 times. 8 stitches remain.

Round 7: (k2t) 4 times. 4 stitches remain.

Cut the yarn and thread through remaining stitches. Finish as given for full size socks.

Miniature Garter Stitch Common Wedge Toe: *Used for Timberline Toes (or as an option for Mermaid)*

Start the toe at one side of the sock. Place markers at either side as given.

(Change to a smaller needle for the Mermaid sock.)

Round 1: (K1, ssk, k6, k2t, k1) twice. 20 stitches remain.

Rounds 2, 4 and 6: Purl.

Round 3: (K1, ssk, k4, k2t, k1) twice. 16 stitches remain.

Round 5: (K1, ssk, k2, k2t, k1) twice. 12 stitches remain.

Graft the remaining stitches and complete as given for full-size socks.

Note: *For a Stocking Stitch Common Wedge Toe, work as above, but knit Rounds 2, 4 and 6.*

Modified Crenellated Edge: *May be used for Crenellated Socks*

The crenellations of this edge have been shortened and their frequency increased to be more in keeping with the scale of the miniature sock.

Bind off 2 stitches, cast on 3 stitches, bind off 4 stitches, repeat.

Miniature socks on page 60:
Starting with the Yellow Zig-Zag at top and moving clockwise:
Simply Splendid: Channel Island Cast-On, Common Heel, Stocking Stitch Wedge Toe. Chequerboard: Garter Stitch Short Row Heel and Toe, 2 x 2 checks, Grafted Textured Chequerboard Cuff. Chequerboard: Garter Stitch Short Row Heel and Toe, 3 x 3 checks, Grafted Textured Chequerboard Cuff. Simply Splendid: Channel Island Cast On, Common Heel, Stocking Stitch Wedge Toe. Simply Splendid: Channel Island Cast On, Common Heel (reinforced), Stocking Stitch Wedge Toe (reinforced). Chequerboard: Garter Stitch Short Row Heel and Toe, yarn dictated checks, Textured Chequerboard Cuff (bound off and sewn).

Miniature Sock Zig-Zag Leg Pattern:
The yellow miniature sock pictured has a two-colour-per-round pattern. A solid colour yarn has been used as background with a self-striping yarn for the contrast.

The pattern has a 6 stitch, 4 row repeat.

Spare Parts for Your Ultimate Socks

The sock patterns in *Cool Socks Warm Feet* consist of a selection of constituent parts. Within certain limitations, they can be swapped about and used in different combinations to create hybrid socks of your own. To make your ultimate sock, use your favourite toe, heel and cuff combinations, coupled with background stitches of your choice. Various sock parts are discussed below with a list of their relative merits and constraints. A few extra sock parts have also been included, for although they were not all used in our Six Exceptional Sock Patterns, they are exceedingly useful, pleasing or fun.

This book is already several times larger (and a year longer) than originally anticipated and it is by no means a comprehensive selection of toes, heels and techniques. For further ideas, techniques or simply inspiration I offer the titles in the bibliography. Never stop experimenting, there is always something new to discover!

Toe-Up Toes

Toe-up socks offer many advantages to the discerning knitter. They include the comfort of working up the leg, knowing that there is sufficient yarn for the second sock (if working an Afterthough or Turkish Heel, complete or reserve yarn for this purpose before binding off at the half-way point of your yarn supply). They also provide the satisfaction of leaving minimal leftover yarn.

For those who loathe grafting (the wonderful Toe-Chimney method notwithstanding, *see page 117),* no grafting is required with these toe-up starts. If coupled with a Garter Stitch Short Row Heel (or other short row heel method of your choice), they ENTIRELY ELIMINATE THE NECESSITY TO GRAFT ANYWHERE IN THE SOCK!

There are many other toe-up methods. Check the bibliography for further reading.

Bosnian-style Garter Stitch Square Toe (see Crenellated Socks)

This is an easy way to begin a toe-up sock. It is not necessary to know the exact number of stitches your sock foot will require before you begin. A gauge swatch is unnecessary, provided the knit fabric is dense. Minimal finishing is required. The toe is symmetrical, the alignment is simply aesthetic and can be set once the toe increases are complete. The size of the initial toe square may be adjusted to suit the weight of yarn and size of the sock. Follow the method given in the *Crenellated Socks* and tailor the number of stitches initially cast on as you deem appropriate.

To give an idea of approximate proportions, the toe square should measure between 2 cm/¾" (for a child's sock), and 4 cm/1½" for an adult sock. The number of stitches knitted up around the toe square is four times the initial number cast on. This resulting number should be between half and two-thirds of the size you estimate for the full-width sock. For example; for an estimated 60-stitch sock, 36-40 stitches would be a good number of stitches on completion of the toe. Thus, a toe square with nine or ten stitches cast on would be ideal. This toe is very forgiving and the numbers are extremely fudgeable (although not good to eat).

PROS

- Easy to start and set up on four or five needles.
- Easily adjusted for a good fit.

- No need to know in advance the precise number of sock stitches.
- Unusual appearance.
- Garter Stitch fabric gives a strong toe.
- No grafting is required to complete the toe.
- Minimal finishing required.
- Once you are familiar with the method, it is easy to work without written directions.

CONS

- Unusual appearance.
- Scattered increases initially delay the start of any set pattern for the foot.

Short Row Toe - Stocking Stitch and Garter

Short Row Toes are logical and fun. They are initially worked flat, to and fro on two or three needles, in a series of decreasing length rows. The unworked stitches are reserved on the needle on either side. The shapings are then reversed to create the second side of the seamless toe. This is an excellent opportunity to practice your short row technique before tackling the Garter Stitch Short Row Heel, as only the toe stitches are on the needles at this point.

The toe is flat and must be positioned with the shaped sides at the sides of the foot of the sock. It is necessary to know how many stitches you wish to have for your sock foot before you begin this toe. If you wish to create customised left and right toes, either toe can be worked asymmetrically. The garter stitch version has the benefit of great elasticity and increased fabric thickness to give a more resilient toe, although the condensed nature of the garter stitch makes the toe somewhat shorter than usual.

The stocking stitch toe is smoother in appearance and more closely resembles a conventional toe.

Garter Stitch Short Row Toe

(see Chequerboard Socks)

PROS

- A thick, elastic, resilient fabric for the toe.
- Smart seamless appearance.
- No grafting.
- Easy to work short rows as they are completed at the start of the sock.
- Easy to set up the needles into round knitting.
- Minimal finishing required.
- Suits any number of stitches.

CONS

- Due to the vertically condensed nature of the garter stitch, the toe is fairly short and stubby.
- You need to know the desired number of stitches for the sock.
- The toe needs to be aligned with the sides of the sock.

Stocking Stitch Short Row Toe

Onto a single gauge-size dpn, and using contrasting WY, use the Provisional Crochet Cast-On. Cast on half of the desired number of stitches for your size, less 1. For example, for an 80 stitch sock, cast on 39 stitches.

Row 1: With sock yarn, purl.

Row 2: S1, knit to last stitch, slip the last stitch to the RHN.

Row 3: Wyif s1, take the working yarn around the outside of the slipped stitch and between the needles, purl to last stitch, slip the last stitch to the RHN.

(The first stitch of the row now has a wrap of yarn around it.)

Row 4: Wyib s1, take the working yarn around the outside of the slipped stitch and between the needles, knit to 2 stitches before the end, SWR, turn.

Row 5: Purl to 2 stitches before the end, SWR. Turn.

Row 6: (RS) Knit to 3 stitches before the end, SWR. Turn.

Row 7: (WS) Purl to 3 stitches before the end, SWR. Turn.

Repeat Rows 6 and 7, leaving one more stitch unworked on each successive pair of rows.

Shapings may be further refined by working later pairs of rows leaving two extra stitches unworked, as the tip of the toe shape is reached.

End with a WS row.

There should be an equal number of stitches with yarn wrapped around them on either side, and the fabric should be "hill" shaped.

Smoothing Rows ** *See note below for further refinements.*

RS: Knit from this mid-row position to the end of the row.

WS: S1, purl to end.

Reverse the short rows as follows (match the new wrapped stitches to the first completed set of wrapped stitches).

RS: S1, knit up to, but not including, the first wrapped stitch beyond the mid-point of the toe, SWR. Turn.

WS: Purl to the first wrapped stitch, SWR. Turn.

RS: Knit to the next wrapped stitch, SWR. Turn.

WS: Purl to the next wrapped stitch, SWR. Turn.

Repeat the last two rows until the last and first stitches of the toe have been wrapped, the toe is completed with a WS row.

Commence knitting in the round. With RS facing and the first stitch slipped and wrapped, knit the first half (approximately as this is likely to be an odd number) of the toe stitches onto one needle. Onto a new needle, knit the remainder plus one stitch knit up from the side of the toe. Unpick the PCCO edge and knit the resulting loops up onto the third and fourth needles, then knit up one or two more stitches, as necessary, at the far side of the sock.

If further adjustment of the stitch numbers is needed, remedy this on the next round. From this point, continue to knit your sock (or mitten!) as usual.

**Connoisseurs may wish to use needles one size larger for the sides of the smoothing rows (or to work the stitches that are knitted into the short rows, rather more loosely than usual). This helps to reduce puckering at the sides of the toe caused by working regular-width stitches along the diagonal edge (the hypotenuse of the toe).

As described above, the wraps of yarn are left on the public side of the work. These wraps do not detract from the appearance of the toe and aid in matching the second set of short rows. However, if you wish to make them vanish, knit or purl (as appropriate) into both the wrap around the stitch and the stitch together on the smoothing rows and each time that you work into a wrapped stitches from the previous row as you reverse the short rows.

Pros

- Smart, seamless appearance.
- Thin, smooth fabric.
- No grafting.
- Easy to work short rows, as they are completed at the start of the sock.
- Easy to set up the needles for round knitting.
- Minimal finishing required.
- Suited to any number of stitches.

Cons

- You need to know the desired number of stitches for the sock.
- Thin toe fabric, therefore slightly more prone to wear.
- Little lengthwise elasticity.
- Flat toe needs to be aligned with the sides of the sock.

Top-Down Toes

These are some of the most frequently used sock toes. Top-down toes are convenient as the knitter can precisely check the required foot length and tailor the shapings accordingly. The frequency of the shapings can be adjusted to suit the future wearer's toes.

Stocking Stitch Common Wedge Toe *(see Simply Splendid and Marietta Rib Socks)*
This is a stocking stitch fabric, on any multiple of four stitches. Stocking stitch is a thin fabric for this heavy wear location, so consider reinforcing the toe as described in *Tip #3, page 7* to produce a thicker fabric.

Garter Stitch Common Wedge Toe *(see Timberline Toes and Mermaid Socks, alternate toe)*
This toe can be made in any multiple of four stitches. It is shorter in length than stocking stitch toes, but may be adjusted by reducing the frequency of decreases.

Pros

- Sock foot length can be fine-tuned at the toes.
- Easy to work.
- Any multiple of four stitches.
- Easy to replace if worn through.

- Suits feet with fairly even length toes.

CONS

- Flat toe needs to be aligned with the sides of the sock.
- Grafting is required for completion.
- The lines of decreases can sometimes stretch apart, revealing ladders.

The Round Toe

This form of toe offers some advantages over the wedge toe. For one, the decreases are spread around the sock circumference, thereby sidestepping the sometimes unsightly stretching between the decrease lines that can occur. This fault is especially noticeable in single-yarn socks. Round toes look good worked in a contrasting colour on a plain sock, but are tricky in a patterned sock unless you line up decreases as in a tam pattern.

A round toe can be made on socks with a multiple of eight stitches. If necessary, make evenly spaced k2t decreases during a single round to bring the sock to a multiple of eight stitches just before starting the toe.

First decrease round: (K6, k2t) repeat to end of round.

Work 5 rounds without shaping.

Second decrease round: (K5, k2t) repeat to end of round.

Work 4 rounds without shaping.

Continue in this manner, working one fewer stitch between decrease positions and one round less between each set of decreases, until the decrease round is (k2t) repeat. One stitch remains of each original eight stitch segment. End the toe by threading the stitches onto the yarn tail as for the *Mermaid Socks.*

The frequency of decrease rounds can be adjusted to suit the future wearer's toes. For socks with less than 64 stitches, or worked in thicker yarns, begin the shaping with the second or third decrease round. Otherwise, the toe will be very long.

PROS

- Doesn't need to be aligned with the foot.
- Informal, with a less geometric appearance.
- No grafting required.
- Suits feet with pointy toes!

CONS

- Fancy patterns usually have to be discontinued once shapings begin.

- A multiple of eight stitches is required, though this usually can be achieved easily.

Heels

Heels that are set in between rounds of knitting, such as the Turkish and Garter Stitch Short Row, are usually set in across 50% of a round's stitches. These socks fold nicely, but I prefer the fit when the opening for the heel is larger. Consider a rigid cardboard tube and imagine cutting across it and halfway through. Would the tube now be inclined to bend easily? No. It is still a rigid structure and, if bent, the corners would tear at each end of the cut.

However, if we were to cut just a little deeper, the tube would bend much more willingly and, in the case of a sock, would create a bigger opening for a fuller heel.

Garter Stitch Short Row Heel

(see Timberline, Chequerboard and Mermaid Socks)

This is a very versatile heel. With a little practice it is easy to set into virtually any sock. For peace of mind, be sure to make a habit of checking the number of wrapped stitches on either side after each pair of heel rows. This method may be used in toe-up or top-down situations on any number of stitches. It causes very little distortion to the sock or disturbance of patterning. This heel has the neatest corners of any heel I know and requires minimal finishing and no grafting. It looks very neat in self-striping yarns and it gives a mitred look, as compared with the concentric rings of the Turkish Heel. (Compare the heels of the *Timberline* and the *Chequerboard* with those of the *Crenellated*.)

When this heel is worked using a separate piece of yarn (which incidentally gives the smartest corners), the stripe pattern of the main body of the sock will remain undisturbed before and after the heel. No yarn from the main ball is used and the stitch count remains the same before and after. Hence, any established sequence of stripes will continue unbroken.

If it is necessary to replace this heel later, it can be cut away leaving the sock tube intact. The resulting sock stitches below can be re-heeled with another short row heel, grafting it into place at the top, or by using both the stitches and loops it can be treated as the opening for a Turkish Heel.

PROS

- Fits neatly into the sock; no gaps anywhere.
- Works for any number of stitches.
- Since the heel is inserted as the sock tube is worked, the sock may be tested for fit at any point.
- Little finishing and no grafting required.
- Warm, durable and well cushioned by the Garter Stitch.
- Easy to work, with little math involved.
- Works for toe-up and top-down socks.
- Looks smart and has an interesting pattern in a self-striping yarn.
- Doesn't alter the number of stitches in the basic sock tube, therefore the main pattern remains unchanged.
- Replaceable.
- May be worked in the main sock yarn or in a contrasting colour if you are husbanding your yarn supply or wish to make a reinforced heel with a different yarn blend.
- The seriously manic sock knitter should note that the heel is worked to and fro, making possible the use of Garter Stitch intarsia patterns within the heel area.

CONS

- There are rather a lot of needles flying around when you work your first heel. Practice setting a heel into a flat swatch before tackling one directly into the sock.
- Looks somewhat different from the rest of the sock.
- Heel depth is slightly shorter than usual, although this is compensated for by the wider opening and the lengthwise elasticity of the Garter Stitch.
- Requires a separate piece of yarn for the heel. If you're working from the centre of the ball, this length may be taken from the outside or vice versa, though it can create a bit of a cat's cradle tangle!

Turkish, Afterthought or Peasant Heel (see *Crenellated Socks*)

Here you have a popular, practical heel. It is essentially a sock toe (most commonly the Common Wedge Toe) that is located at the heel and worked last, being inserted into the sock tube after the main sock knitting has been completed. The opening for the heel may be preplanned by setting in WY at the appropriate position, or created later by snipping a thread at the centre back of the sock and unpicking the necessary number of stitches in both directions. The set in of the heel is slightly neater if preplanned. This heel may be used in either direction, with matching or contrasting yarn, in stocking or garter stitch. The sock may be tested for fit to tailor the heel shapings.

PROS

- Works for any number of stitches.
- Warm, durable and well cushioned by the Garter Stitch version.
- Easy to work, with only four needles in the work and little math involved.
- Works for toe-up and top-down socks.
- Has an interesting bull's eye pattern in a self-striping yarn.
- Doesn't alter the number of stitches in the basic sock tube, so the basic pattern remains unchanged.
- Replaceable.
- May be worked in the main sock yarn or a contrasting colour if you are husbanding your yarn supply or wish to make a reinforced heel with a different yarn blend.

- The heel blends in with the rest of the sock.

CONS

- Rather ragged corners require some nimble needlework to fully beautify, and the final closure is a graft.
- Sock fit cannot be checked until the heel is opened.
- Heel depth is slightly shorter than usual, although this is compensated for by the wider opening.
- When working stranded knitting (two-colours-per-round) or a pattern involving decreases, work the first round above the WY in one yarn only, in plain stocking stitch. It is hard to find the loops between the stitches above the heel otherwise.

Common Heel (see Simply Splendid Socks)
A well-fitting, practical heel, tried, tested and true. A traditional favourite of many knitters, although it tends to slow some down because of the number of stages required.

This is a sophisticated heel, as each stage offers a selection of opportunities for the knitter to customize the fit of the sock (see page 94). Of course, with each opportunity comes the need to make a decision.

Once you have worked a few heels by this method and can see the inter-relationship of the various stages and figures, there is no further need to slavishly follow a pattern.

For socks made with printed yarns, the Common Heel has a mainly aesthetic drawback — the heel flap, short rows and decreasing rounds all use varying amounts of yarn. This disturbs the pattern of a repetitively striping yarn and can make designing a fancy patterned sock quite challenging.

PROS

- The ultimate heel for adaptation, customization and adjustment.
- May be worked in the Main sock yarn or a contrasting colour if you are husbanding your yarn supply or wish to make a reinforced heel with a different yarn blend, although it doesn't make as neat a transition as the set in heels.
- The distinct areas of the sock offer design opportunities to introduce different patterns and stitches.

CONS

- A multi-stage, though not complex, operation, requiring the attention of the knitter.

- The fabric should be reinforced when working the short row section of turning the heel.
- Gappy corners require some needlework to fully beautify.
- Disturbs the number of stitches, thus altering the appearance of self-striping yarns.
- This is a one-directional heel for top-down socks.

Top-Down Cuffs

There are so many ways to avoid the classic "cast on and rib until you can stand it no longer" cuffs. Here are a few suggestions.

One of the major advantages of over-sized sock tops is the total elimination of the possibility of a tight edge to your sock. Don't struggle to get all the stitches for ruffles and scallops onto your set of needles; use a 40 cm/16" needle for the over-sized rounds, and change to the sock needles when the numbers become more reasonable.

Ruffled Turn-Over Top (see *Marietta Rib pattern for full details*)

For every 3 stitches required (round upwards), cast on 7 stitches.

So for 76 stitch sock: 76/3 = 25 groups of 3 + 1 odd stitch, therefore cast on 26 x 7 sts = 182 sts.

On completion of the Ruffle, make any necessary adjustments to the stitch numbers.

Scalloped Turn-Over Top (see Marietta Rib pattern for full details)

For every 4 stitches required, cast on 10 stitches.

So for 76 stitch sock: 76/4 = 19 groups of 4, cast on 19 x 10 sts = 190 sts.

Latvian Twist Edging

This is a fun edging with which to begin a sock. I discovered it on a pair of contemporary socks purchased in Latvia by a friend. This edging cannot be made in the round, as it requires twists in the cast-on edge. For a sock (or mitten), work the edging with selvage stitches, complete the twisting round, then commence knitting in the round, decreasing away the selvage stitches.

For maximum visual impact, make the cast-on edge in your brightest colour with a strongly contrasting stripe adjacent to it. With a self-striping yarn, you can either let the yarn take its own course or arrange the rows so that the cast-on edge,

and subsequent pairs of rows are essentially single-coloured (cutting out yarn may be necessary), or use odds and ends of solid colour yarns for the edging before launching into the Main yarn.

As this edging alone is not enough to fully stabilize an edge, follow it with some non-curling stitch pattern.

With Colour A, long tail cast on any multiple of 5 stitches + 12.

With Colour B, knit 2 rows.

With Colour C, knit 2 rows.

With Main colour yarn, k6, (push the LHN away from you and down underneath the cast on edge at the front of the work and continue to rotate the needle until it regains its working position, *the twist created in the edge should fall between the needles*, k5) repeat; end (twist, k6).

Finish off with any non-curling stitch, such as garter, rib, moss or seed.

For an 80-stitch sock, add two selvage stitches; 82 sts = (14 x 5) + 12. As this edge limits you to 62, 67, 72, 77 or any number of stitches ending with a 7 or 2, work the edging oversized and decrease away the extra stitches later. For this example, work edging on 82 stitches and then decrease to 80.

This edging is very versatile. It looks good in a single colour, and the distance between twists and the direction of the twist can be varied, or arranged as a pattern.

PROS

- A pretty and unusual edging.
- Easy to knit.

CONS

- You have to seam together the first few rounds and hide a few yarn tails.

Sideways Garter Stitch Cuff (see Mermaid Socks)

This cuff is an entertaining method of sizing any top-down ankle sock, eliminating the need to swatch. The number of stitches required for your size of sock will be determined by the number of rows in the cuff. Simply work a firm garter stitch fabric (the row length should be the desired height of the cuff), until it fits the ankle of the intended wearer. For stocking stitch socks, aim for a snug fit. With Mermaid Socks only, aim for a gentle fit.

Garter stitch has a delightful property — the vertical height of two rows of garter stitch equals the width of one stitch when worked by the same knitter with the same needles and yarn.

Therefore, when you knit up one stitch along one edge of the cuff for every garter ridge, you end up with the number of stitches you need for your ankle measurement. This takes into account your personal tension, choice of yarn and needles. Before knitting-up the sock stitches, you may join the cuff by seaming the two ends together. Or, if you enjoy grafting, you may unite the ends invisibly with a perfect graft. By completing the knitting one row short of the final repeat, the stitch tops of the last row worked can be connected flawlessly to the bottoms of the first row of stitches, and the sewn row of stitches will complete the last repeat. With stitch-top to stitch-bottom grafts, there is no misalignment of the columns of stitches.

PROS

- This is an interesting way to start a sock. All you need is the future wearer's ankle measurement.
- No need to swatch.
- Adds a pleasing vertical element to a sock leg. Alternating two colours for each pair of rows or using self-striping yarn further emphasizes this aspect.
- If grafted, the cuff makes an interesting puzzle for another knitter to work out how you achieved this result!

CONS

- It is necessary to seam or graft the cuff together.

Toe-Up Cuffs

One of the biggest issues of toe-up socks is how best to dispose of the stitches at the ankle. Frequently, the bound-off edge is too tight or, if it is worked very loosely, looks messy.

2 x 2 Rib with Expanded Bind-Off (see Crenellated Socks, Option 3)

For a relaxed edge yet plain appearance, work the final round of 2 x 2 rib as follows:

(k1, m1, k1, p2) repeat.

Bind off in (k3, p2) rib.

The increase round results in a 25% increase in the number of stitches. This effectively prevents the possibility of a tight edge, with little outward change in the appearance of the rib.

PROS

- Neat, easy and unobtrusive in a 2 x 2 rib.

CONS

- This method isn't quite as easy to place in a 1 x 1 rib.
- For a 1 x 1 rib, substitute a crochet hook for the RHN and work: (bind off two stitches [a k/p pair], make a single crochet chain into the one stitch on the hook), repeat.

Picot Bind-Off/Cast-On (see Crenellated Socks, Option 2)

This is a method of creating a decorative edge with little bumps or tails. It also gives the edge a little more elasticity.

As a bound-off edge: Bind off a number of stitches, ** return the single stitch remaining on the RHN to the LHN and cast on a few new stitches by knitting into the loop. These new stitches form the length of the Picot. Bind off the new stitches plus a few more. The number of additional bound-off stitches determines the spacing of the picots. Repeat from **.

As a cast-on edge: **Cast on a number of stitches to include the space and picot length (by the method previously given), bind off a number of stitches (these bound-off stitches form the length of the Picot), return the single stitch remaining on the RHN to the LHN. Repeat from **.

As you can see, the spacing and length of each picot is very flexible. For blunt picots, knit the first stitch to be bound off. For rounder tips, slip the first stitch, knit the second and bind off as before. If you wish to avoid the slight gap between the two sides of the picot at the cast-on edge, the final stitch can be passed over the last stitch on the LHN before continuing.

PROS

- Adds elasticity to the edge.
- Very decorative.
- Spacing and picot length can be scaled to suit the size of the project.

CONS

- Quite slow to set up.
- Creates slight gaps between the stitches when casting on, although these are controlled by the next round of stitches.

Facings for Toe-Up Socks - *See Facings section below.*

Top Down Cast-On Methods

Picot Cast-On - *see Toe-Up Cuffs*

Tubular Cast-On *(see page 111)*

PROS

- Suits both 2 x 2 and 1 x 1 Ribs.
- Pleasing, rounded edge with no visible cast on line.
- A tubular channel in the edge can be used for elastic.

CONS

- It is tempting to use too small a needle initially, thus giving a tight edge.
- Slow to establish but worth the effort.

Long Tail or Continental Cast-On *(see page 105)*

PROS

- Very useful, general purpose cast on method.
- Spacing of the stitches can be controlled to give an elastic edge.

CONS

- Has a different appearance on each side.

Channel Island Cast-On *(see page 108)*

PROS

- Very handsome edge with rounded picot-type points.
- Very good elasticity.

CONS

- Limited in application, best suited to 1 x 1 rib or Garter Stitch.
- Tricky to start and establish even stitches, but worth the effort.

Facings: Top-Down and Toe-Up

A knitted-in facing is an excellent start to a top-down sock. It stabilizes the upper edge without restricting the elasticity with a cast-on edge. In addition, facings can be used to protect long, loose floats of yarn between lettering from snagging, or to cushion the wearer from beads.

The internal layer of the facing needs to be a little smaller than the external layer if you wish to avoid puckering and flaring of the sock top. There are two main ways to achieve this. Either work the facing on an equal number of stitches using smaller needles, or work on fewer stitches with the same needle size (usually 10% fewer, e.g. 72 stitches for an 80-stitch sock).

For knitters already using their smallest needles the only option is to reduce the number of stitches in the facing.

For either style of facing, cast on using the PCCO method (use 10% fewer stitches if not adjusting needle size). A provisional cast-on is used to completely avoid the restrictions of a cast-on edge.

Beginning at the unravelable edge of your PCCO, work your inner lining fabric, usually stocking stitch (being a smooth, thin fabric), for the desired length (from ½ to 1 inch, according to taste).

Work one further round, increasing stitches to the full number, if necessary.

Make one or more *turning rounds*, changing to the gauge needle size, if necessary. (A *turning round* is an interruption to the stocking stitch fabric, which will cause a neat fold at this point.)

Possible options for turning rounds include: one round of reverse stocking stitch (purl one round) to give a sharp crease line; two or three rounds of reverse stocking stitch (purl rounds) for a progressively softer fold; or one round of (0, k2t) repeat, which will result in decorative peaks once folded.

Continue the public face of the sock cuff as desired until the stitches on the needle are level with the lower edges of the stitches of the facing when folded. Keep on checking to get the best match.

Darn any tails within the facing at this point, as they will be inaccessible after the facing has been joined.

Now join the facing to the exterior fabric. This is achieved most easily on a plain knit round. Fold the facing up inside the cuff. Unravel the PCCO from the chain end, stitch by stitch as needed; knit the next stitch on the working needle together with a released loop from the PCCO edge; repeat this for every stitch for facings with the same number of stitches. For socks with a smaller number of stitches in the facing, work one exterior stitch unpaired every 1/10th of the round. Every eighth stitch would be unpaired in the example given.

The facing is now complete, joined and free of any restrictive edge.

For toe-up socks the situation is reversed. Work as usual up to the turning round(s), reduce the number of stitches or needle size and work the facing to an approximately equal length. Cut off the yarn with a tail long enough for one more round. Slip the live stitches onto a contrasting thread.

Turn the sock inside out, neaten any ends to be encased by the facing, and then secure each of the live stitches to the inside of the sock; they may be very gently stitched in place or, better yet, semi-grafted to maintain maximum elasticity. *See Diagram 11.*

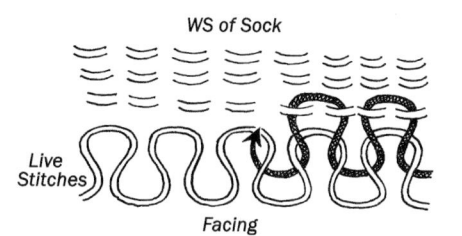

Diagram 11 illustrates the semi-grafting of a facing to the inside of a sock.

See *Crenellated Socks, Option 4 (see page 33) for Rib facing details.*

PROS

- A very elegant solution to tight sock tops.

CONS

- Facings increase the thickness of the sock cuff.

Techniques, Tactics and Tools of the Trade

Sock Needles

All knitters have their own preference regarding the needles they select for particular types of projects.

A variety of factors determine which needles will suit you best.

Needle Materials

The performance and feel of a needle is very different according to the material from which it is made. All needles offer unique properties. The weight of the needle is very significant, especially in the larger sizes. Solid metal needles are heavy and have the tendency to cause loud clanking sounds as you work. They are also frequently (and noisily) overcome by the forces of gravity, especially when operated with only a few stitches or while casting on. Lighter needles, made from birch wood, bamboo or casein, are a joy to use. Needles that don't conduct heat are best for use near ice rinks! For "demolition" style knitters, metal needles are the least likely to break or splinter, although some brands of bamboo needles are remarkably resilient. In larger sizes, birch wood needles are delightfully light and easy. For finer sizes, good quality resin-impregnated bamboo needles are pleasantly rigid, slick and well-pointed.

Friction and Flex

The surface coating or material used in the needle directly affects the friction of the stitches on the needle. For fine socks in particular, it is helpful to have a very slick needle. Nickel-plated brass circulars are the sleekest. The quality of the join between the needle and the flexible section is paramount; if possible, check this join before purchasing, or ask for advice. The flexibility of the material can make a significant difference to your comfort; plastic and casein needles with some yield may be kinder to delicate hands. Experiment with a variety of types and makes until you experience needle nirvana.

The colour of needles can also be significant. Dark needles show off light stitches. Sets of matching colour (or colour-coded) needles can help you to avoid using odd pins inadvertently. Shiny nickel-plated needles are best used out of the sun — the glare can be fierce!

Tip Shape

Different brands of needles have different styles of tips. For fine socks, a slender tip with a nice taper (neither too abrupt nor too shallow) is helpful, particularly when decreasing. If you push on the tips of the needles as you knit, you may prefer blunter needles (or slicker needles that slide through the stitches more easily) to avoid finger damage. As with all other aspects of needle choice, don't give up. If you don't like the needles you are using, try another brand. Guilds and Internet knit groups are largely free of commercial bias and are great places to canvass opinion on these subjects.

Needle tips have a significant effect on the style of your knitting. Many experienced knitters have never analyzed their knitting technique since the day they first cast on. Remember how the terror of lost stitches kept us ramming the stitches further up the needles? It is time to relax; we no longer feel faint at the thought of a lost stitch. Try working nearer to the tips of your needles. These calibrated stitch-measuring tools (needles) are designed to measure a unit of yarn thrown around the needle at its full width.

When working with two needles in a single stitch or a pair of stitches (for a decrease), try to keep only the tip or tapered section of each needle in the stitches. Once the yarn is drawn through the old stitch, then it's time to slide the right-hand needle into it, so that the stitch is wrapped around the full circumference of the needle. Now withdraw the needle, so that the stitch can be

near the tip again before working the next stitch. Not only will this tidy up some irregularities in stitches, it will also make your knitting a little more efficient, as your hands and fingers won't have so far to travel.

Needle Size

Smaller, smaller, smaller.

Socks should be worked on abnormally small needles for the size of yarn.

The most common failing of sock knitters is using too large a needle size for the chosen yarn. Yarn producers tend to suggest larger needle sizes on their ball bands than are ideal for socks. That is true even on yarns that we consider to be specifically spun for this purpose. The producers can be forgiven. They have no way of knowing your personal knitting tension and whether you intend a lace shawl, a stocking stitch sweater or enduring socks. Yarn producers are in the business of selling yarn. They do not wish to further endanger the global population of knitters by causing them heart failure when they read the suggested needle size on the label. Knitters can knit faster and consume more yarn at looser gauges, and it is of little concern to anyone other than yourself whether your sock lasts one year or five.

A slack sock may look perfectly lovely as it comes off the needles, but once it is worn and begins to stretch, the weaknesses begin to show, and it rapidly becomes a droopy string-bag for over-foot wear.

Look for brands of needles that offer many small size increments, 2, 2.25, 2.5, 2.75, 3 mm (# 0, 1, 1½, 2, 2½ US). This range offers the knitter much more versatility than 2, 2.5, and 3 mm or # 0, 1, 2 US. A quarter millimetre difference in needle diameter makes a big difference to the stitch size, especially at this end of the needle range.

Finely knit socks (and any other kind of knitting) simply look smarter and more polished. We are not in a race. And, you'll get much more knitting pleasure for your money!

Single yarn socks should be knit as tightly as possible. Stranded socks (with two colours per round) can be knit on slightly larger needle sizes. If working a sock with bands of stranded and plain fabric, change to a larger needle size at the junction of the two-colour bands. This will counteract the gathering effect of the stranded sections. *See Tip 14, page 8.*

The body of the Mermaid Socks is knit on larger needles than the heels or toes, as the stitches twist round on the diagonal and would otherwise gather the sock in.

✓ For sock knitting, use as small a needle size as you comfortably can. The firmer the fabric produced, the longer the sock will last. It will wear well and recover its shape after washing, donning or doffing.

Rigid or Flexible Double-Pointed?

Worldwide, for hundreds of years, socks have been worked on sets of four or five short, straight needles with points at either end, known as double-pointed needles. Metal needles became less expensive and more widely available with the advent of drawn plate wire during the reign of Queen Elizabeth I (1558-1603) and have changed little since then. These simple needles were easy to make or improvise.

The advent of more sophisticated manufacturing methods is spawning a new breed of sock knitters, those who prefer to use one, two (or more) circular needles instead of rigid, double-pointed needles.

Regardless of the type you choose, buy the best quality needles you can afford; you will spend a lot of time handling them and, with reasonable care, they can last a lifetime.

Rigid Double-Pointed Needles

Short rigid, double-pointed needles remain my favourites for fine sock knitting. I enjoy a set of five bamboo double-pointed needles, six inches long.

Choosing Rigid Double-Pointed Needles

When working on a set of double-pointed needles, consider the needle length; there are a variety of lengths available, from four inches to ten inches long. Eight-inch needles have been a standard for many years; they are well-suited to larger projects, such as bulky socks or hat crowns. For fine socks, six-inch needles offer plenty of working room without the resting stitches being in danger of falling off the tips. Matching project size with needle length eliminates a quiverful of unused needle ends flying around.

Shorter, four-or five-inch-long needles are also available. These are more usually used for glove fingers. Some knitters love them, while others find them too short and uncomfortable to use for long periods.

Four-Needle Sets or Five?

Generations of great knitters have been raised using only sets of four needles. Certain brands of needles are packaged in this way, especially in the U.K. and U.S. Check the packet carefully when purchasing! Five-needle sets offer many advantages:

- When there are three needles in the work, each corner of the sock has to bend sharply. When there are four needles in the work the angles are softened, lessening the tendency for laddered or distorted corners.
- This reduced corner angle also makes it easy to circulate your stitches from needle to needle, thus altering the "corner" positions periodically, and helping to ward off problems with distortion and ladders at these locations.
- The additional needle also makes a handy temporary parking place for various sections of the sock stitches, especially when turning the heel.
- If one needle is lost overboard, it is possible to continue working.
- A sock on four needles is easy to fold flat for travel. The fabric of the sock can then be rolled around the four needles and the fifth needle used as a skewer to fasten the whole sushi sock roll. A needle point protector can then be slipped over all five of the needle tips (one cup at each end), to hold the stitches

securely. Pairs of point protectors linked with an elastic cord are very handy.

✓ When working in the round with double-pointed needles, help avoid baggy or laddered "corners" by moving or circulating your stitches around at your convenience. This is easiest on a set of five needles. When a needle is empty, work an extra one or two stitches onto the old working needle as before (only four needles working at this point), then introduce the empty needle and proceed as usual. This may be repeated each time a needle is empty. It is not compulsory to have equal numbers of stitches on all needles at all times. Markers can be used to keep track of important positions in the round. Stitches may also be slipped unworked from one needle to another. On some occasions, this may be made easier by using an extra needle.

Storing Double-Pointed Needles

For large collections, pocketed double-pointed needle holders are great, especially if they offer wider pockets for thicker needles and a variety of pocket depths for different needle lengths.

I also keep a mug full of needles by my knitting chair. It's cushioned with a little fabric in the bottom to prevent damage to the tips of loose needles. Full sets of needles are held together with point protectors.

Some brands of needles are stamped or etched with the size. When they aren't, I colour code them with a number of stripes (relating to the needle size), made with an indelible pen. It is helpful to keep a needle gauge handy for sorting out unmarked needles.

Flexible Double-Pointed Needles, Also Known As Circulars

The most important factor with circular needles is the quality of the join between the flexible nylon cord and the rigid needle ends. Heavenly knitting can be quickly transformed into a refined form of torture if the joint snags.

For those who prefer working in the round on circular needles rather than dpns, very short length (30 cm/12") needles are available. These needles feel a little cramped for some, but they suit others ideally. They have the merit of not needing to change from one working needle to the next and there are no corner issues to be concerned about. The beginning of the round, and other significant positions, can be marked; and ring markers will not drop off this type of needle. The circumference of the sock must be sufficient to stretch comfortably around the needle. There is minimal risk of dropped stitches or lost needles. Using circular needles may also reduce the gathering effect when working two-colour-per-round stitch patterns. The work is very portable with only two needle tips protruding.

Multiple Flexible Double-Pointed Needles

Two (or more) comfortably-long, circular needles can also be used for socks. A portion of the sock stitches is placed on each circular needle. The stitches to be worked are slid to the right-hand end of their needle and then are worked back onto the tail end of the SAME needle by working the stitches, using the opposite end of the needle. On completion of a section of stitches, the newly worked stitches are positioned in the flexible, middle section of the needle before moving on to the next section of stitches.

There is no limitation regarding the length of the needles used; very long needles simply result in a lot of dangling flex. Shorter, yet comfortably-long needles (40-50 cm/16-20") are the favourite lengths for most knitters.

This method of using two circular needles offers longer stretches of unbroken knitting since the work is divided into halves. It also reduces the gathering effect when working two-colour-per-round stitch patterns. As well, none of the

needles are ever empty of stitches, thus reducing the chances of a lost needle. However, the transition from one needle to another can be problematic and may give slight unevenness at these points.

The photograph above illustrates a sock on two circular needles.

A benefit of this technique is that sections of a sock may be worked at differing gauges by using different sizes of needles for the respective stitches; for example, a smaller needle can be used for the sole stitches of a double-knit sole while a larger needle can be used for a stitch pattern that compresses the gauge across the instep.

A circular needle can always be pressed into service to double as a regular, rigid double-pointed needle. It is simply longer and wobbly!

It is also possible to use 3 circular needles as illustrated above.

Storing Circular Needles

For those better organized than I, these needles can be re-coiled, stored in their plastic bags and filed in a shoe-box according to size and length. Sock knitters may prefer to store multiples of sizes together as sets.

For a large number of needles, hanging needle holders with horizontal slots for each needle size are ideal — the advantage is that you can see exactly how many of each size are on hand. Because the needles are stored uncoiled, they don't require de-kinking prior to use. (To de-kink, hold the flexible section in the steam from a kettle or dip it in very hot water.)

For the well-endowed knitter, a separate needle holder for each length of needle is very handy.

Sock Yarns

Yarn Weights

Socks can be knit in any weight of yarn, as most designs are based on a series of proportions, though with the patterns given here, thicker yarn requires some shaping modifications. *See page 93.*

Fit and Function

Fine yarns are popular for socks that will fit comfortably into regular shoes, but many hunters and hikers adore thicker socks. Select strong, durable yarns as socks are subject to extreme conditions, perhaps the most challenging faced by any knitted garment. Socks needs to stretch prodigiously to admit the ankle, then contract back to hug the foot and leg. Then we stuff the whole into a shoe! If this were not enough abuse, to further test the sock, we run, jump and sweat. Repeatedly, *ad infinitum*. This is an ideal environment for felting — warmth, moisture and movement are all present.

Fibre Content

The most popular sock yarns are blends. For warmth, look for wool, and for durability, look for a percentage of nylon or poly-something blended in with the wool — for instance, 75% wool/25% synthetic. Cotton blends with the synthetic content are popular in warmer climes. Most dedicated sock yarns are machine washable, with differing degrees of resultant fluffing. Most are superb. Many yarns will also come smiling through a dryer.

Mohair blend yarns are also very well suited to socks. Mohair is warm, very strong and durable and only mats rather than truly felting, but check the properties of the other fibres used in the blend. Do not overlook other yarns not specifically blended for socks. Simply knit them firmly and use reinforcing techniques. Wash and wear them with respect and bestow them only on those who understand hand-washing.

Skeins and Balls

Most sock yarns come ready-wound into balls. For those yarns that don't, it is most useful to wind them into centre-pull balls, which give easy access to either end of the yarn.

To do this, undo the skein and straighten the yarn. Ensure that the yarn is all leading around in a circle with no strands doubling-back on themselves. With your hands inside the skein at either end, snap the skein taut a couple of times; this helps to release any adhesion between the strands. Place this circular loop of yarn onto a pair of willing hands, a chair back or, best of all an umbrella swift. (A swift is an elegant device for holding skeins of yarn, which rotates as the yarn is unwound. If you anticipate more than occasional use of skeins, a swift is a very worthwhile investment.)

Having mounted your yarn ready to be wound, untie any securing loops and yarn ends. Take one or other end of the skein, whichever seems to lead most easily, and wind the yarn into a ball.

If you have a ball winder, this will automatically make a ball which may be used from either end, but in the absence of such, an empty cardboard tube will suffice. Lodge the end of the yarn in a slit in the top of the tube. Wind around the middle of the tube a couple of times, then angle the tube slightly so that the yarn being wound falls on the diagonal across the first few turns; as you do this, slowly rotate the tube so that the diagonal threads form an evenly balanced pile around the tube. Continue until a couple of yards/metres remain and wrap this straight around the ball and ball band. Tuck the tail in behind. Remove the tube, keeping hold of the yarn tail.

In addition to being able to use either end of the yarn, the removal of the tube allows the yarn to relax in the ball. Relaxed yarn gives more reliable results when swatched and measured without washing.

Pre-wound balls of yarn may usually be used from the centre. Insert your little finger gently into the middle of the ball, feel around to find the hollow core of the ball, then hook a small number of strands with the end of your finger and pull them out through the end of the ball. With a bit of luck, a small clump of yarn will emerge (rather than a full-scale disembowelment), and lurking therein, you should find the end of the yarn. If an even number of strands are connecting the clump of yarn to the ball, the tail is still within the ball.

Always check the fibre blend information and washing instructions on the ball bands.

Printed, Variegated, Space-Dyed and Hand-Painted Yarns

Many of these colourful yarns, when in the ball or skein, do not give the knitter a clue as to how they will look once they have been knit. All that can be determined is that the visible colours will appear in your work at some time or other; but there could also be others hidden deep within the ball. It's an adventure.

Size Matters! The same yarn can give remarkably different results, according to the number of stitches in the round.

If you are determined to know what is going on within, there are a couple of options. Make some deductions based on what you can see, ask to see knitted samples, quiz guild friends or check out the yarn producer's website. Yarns will pattern differently according to the point in the colour sequence where you begin, the number of stitches in your sock, and your tension and needle size.

Once you own the yarn, you are free to unravel a length and get a feel for what is taking place. Are the colour lengths long or short? Are the colour changes abrupt or subtly graded? Can you see a visible repeat? Often it is not practical to unwind a full repeat unless you enjoy untangling vast amounts of confused yarn. The first two properties are really the most important if you plan to make a design to exploit the yarn. (See *Mermaid* and *Chequerboard* patterns, both of which show up most dramatically when worked in yarns with abrupt changes.) Changes are usually more distinct when a variety of strongly contrasting colours can be seen. But this doesn't totally rule out blending between colours!

A yarn composed of many shades of similar colours, such as purples and blues, will show off slightly more complex stitch patterns, than will strongly speckled, striped and wildly contrasting yarns. The eye is far more bewitched by dramatic colours than by textured effects. *See page 21.*

Repeat Length and Directionality

As you work with a particular yarn, you will become familiar with its colour sequence. There are few yarns that do not have some repetitive pattern. The frequency of repetition in your project is based on the length of the yarn used in each row or round. For example, about four rounds if a sweater is being knit, or 16 or more rounds if a sock.

✓ To join a new ball mid-project, you might like to wind off part of your new ball so it begins at the same point in the sequence where the old yarn ceased. To avoid reversing the sequence, work the yarn from the same end of the ball.

For Garter Stitch Short Row Heels worked from a single yarn source, I use the opposite end of the ball to provide the heel yarn. The sequence of colours is therefore reversed in the heel, but as the heel has a sequence of its own, this reversal is not a significant drawback.

Admirers of symmetry may wish to begin each sock from the same point in the colour sequence to keep the two socks as similar as possible. I enjoy variety and am happy with a family resemblance between a pair of socks, so would consider deliberately reversing the direction of yarn usage for the second sock.

The pattern created by a particular yarn is directly related to the amount of yarn used per round, which is a function of the number of stitches, size of needle and tension of the knitter. *See photograph, page 89.* Pieces of knit fabric worked flat (to and fro) will be different again. Keep these factors in mind when looking at sample socks and swatches.

The Common Heel (used in *Simply Splendid Socks*), completely changes the pattern of the yarn until the original number of stitches is regained after turning the heel. The heel flap will make wider stripes. It is worked on half of the original number of stitches, with some stitches slipped every alternate row. After the heel is turned, the rounds are significantly longer than before, so the stripes will be narrower. The yarn used to knit across the reserved instep stitches will now be at a different point in the sequence from when the sock was divided, often causing a distinct colour jump. (*See page 19.*) If this disruption bothers you, this style of sock may be better suited to speckled yarns or short repeats. An alternative approach would be to use an entirely contrasting yarn to work the heel flap and turning rows, and then rejoin the Main yarn for the knit-up round. This will still disturb the pattern, as you have more stitches than before you began the heel. Until the gusset decreases are finished, the stripes will be narrower.

The Turkish and Short Row heels both make attractive and practical heels that interrupt the sequence of the foot considerably less than the conventional ones.

Making the Colours Do Your Bidding

It is fun (and quite legal) to "adjust" the colours and sequence of the yarn by omitting bits here and there if the colours threaten to mess up your pattern. If you wish to keep each unit within a particular colour section of the yarn when working modular patterns, complete a unit, then advance to the next colour as you begin the next unit. Save the annexed lengths of yarn; they may come in handy later for finishing details or may be used as WY. If there are colours lurking within the ball that you find quite loathsome, then simply miss them out!

Colour in Cast-On Edges

Give a little consideration to the point in the yarn colour sequence when you begin your cast on. Great effects can be achieved, especially with yarns that have fairly long lengths of colour. The outcome will vary according to the technique that you favour. It may require experimentation to adjust the starting position to get this exactly as you wish.

To achieve a spectacular cast-on edge with the Long-tail Cast-On method (*see page 105*), begin your cast on at the junction of two colours. First unwind a sufficient length for your long tail until the junction between two promising colour sections is reached. Begin your cast on from this point; the yarn fastening the stitch will be of one colour, and the stitch on the needle another. The extreme edge of the cast on will contrast strikingly with the first row of stitches. This effect was used to emphasize the Scalloped Cast-On edge (*see page 36*).

To guarantee this effect under other yarn conditions, you may also tie two contrasting yarns together and begin your cast on from the knot. Later, remove the knot and hide the evidence!

For Channel Island Cast-On, make the double strand from one single colour. Fold the length of the colour in half, so that your right hand holds the single strand of new colour and the double yarn in the left is different. *See page 21.*

The Latvian Twist Edging (*see pages 21 and 73*) looks most striking when the outer colour is the brightest and when each successive garter ridge is a different colour. (I tinkered with the yarn sequence to force this to happen.) Using the Long-Tail method, the tail length was adjusted to make the entire cast-on edge in a single colour. It took several attempts.

Doing the Bidding of the Colours

There are many entertaining games you can play if you let the yarn dictate how you knit! The result will differ from knitter to knitter. It all depends on how the yarn colour sequence contrives to pattern for your chosen size. Pay attention to the yarn as you work; the changes in the colours will determine the stitches and the colour changes will not necessarily occur at the beginning and end point of the round.

Textured Striping According to the Colour

Knit all the stitches of one or more colours and purl all the stitches of another. Remember that when you purl into a stitch it brings the stitch head of the stitch below to the front of the work. If you wish to keep your stripe colours from bleeding into one another, work the first round of the colour-to-be-purled in knit, before purling thereafter. This will give random, textured patches according to the colour lengths of your yarn.

In the tiger-striped yarn, the black was purled every time a black stitch was worked into with black yarn. This action created periodic partial rounds of black garter ridges (*see page 21*).

The reverse stocking stitch rolls underneath the cuff of the *Mermaid Socks* were determined by the length of the colour sequence. Rather than arbitrarily changing from knit to purl (or vice versa) at the centre back of the sock, the position of the change was determined by the colour of the yarn. To achieve a distinctly-coloured reverse stocking stitch band (every round purl), change to purl one round after the colour changes. To achieve a distinctly coloured stocking stitch band (every round knit), change to knit immediately as the colour changes.

Textural chequerboards can be made with a single, striping yarn. Set up a simple rib pattern which fits into your sock repeat. In that round the knit stitches will show your colours clearly, the purls will blend the colours together. After a couple of rounds and at a convenient colour position in the yarn, knit one round and then reverse the rib. The frequency of reversals can be determined by the colours in the yarn. *See page 21.*

Sock Fit and Adjustment

Most socks are based on a series of ratios and proportions designed to comfortably fit the mythical "average human foot." The *Simply Splendid Socks* and *Marietta Rib Socks* are based on a traditional sock formula, the evergreen popularity of which is a testament to the wide range of feet that it suits and the number of customizing adjustments that can be made to it.

The basic sock formula relies on the wearer having an ankle measurement (measured in the dip just above the ankle bone) very similar to the measurement around the foot after the instep and before the toes. This appears to hold true for the majority of people.

The number of stitches to cast on is based entirely on the ankle measurement. It is a simple multiplication of the ankle size in cm/inches and gauge in stitches per cm/inch. For convenient division the resulting figure is usually rounded up for ribbed socks or down for stocking stitch (or according to taste), to a multiple of four stitches. This can be modified within reason, to suit any necessary constraints posed by a desired pattern repeat.

A useful property of garter stitch is that, at most gauges, the height of two rows of garter stitch equals the width of one stitch of stocking stitch. This property gives an alternative method for sizing a sock with a sideways garter stitch cuff. The garter stitch cuff is knit until it fits snugly around the ankle. It then has the dual function of acting as a gauge swatch and determining the number of stitches needed for the sock while you are working the cuff. Use small needles to give a firm cuff fabric, and work the garter band until it fits the ankle. The number of stitches used for the cuff determines the height of the cuff, as the cuff rows run vertically around the ankle. Graft or seam the beginning of the cuff to the end. Onto this cylinder, with right side facing and one stitch away from the edge, knit up one stitch per garter ridge around the cuff (one garter ridge equals two rows), then proceed as usual, adjusting the stitch numbers downwards as necessary to the nearest multiple of four.

For short socks, the elasticity of the knit fabric takes care of any slight increase in the leg circumference for a few inches above the ankle. For full length socks, other steps need to be taken to accommodate the calf comfortably.

Areas for Adjustment

There are a number of places within a conventional sock where adjustments may be made. Each adjustment has an effect on subsequent sections of the sock.

The Heel Flap

On completion of the leg, the initial number of stitches is divided, half and half, into heel and instep stitches. If necessary, this division can be modified slightly to accommodate patterning attractively — for example, splitting the sock at the midpoint of a 2 x 2 rib on either side.

The heel flap stitches are usually worked in a stitch pattern which compresses the height of the rows (often with slip stitches). This will cause two rows of the heel flap fabric to be approximately the same height as the width of one knit stitch. This is the ratio assumed when knitting up the new stitches along the side of the flap.

The stitch pattern also reduces the width of the flap without altering the number of stitches, so that the back of the sock narrows to fit the back of the ankle better. Slip stitches with firm floats, small cables or firm two-colour-per-row knitting make good heel flaps.

An apparently coincidental benefit from the use of these "condensing" stitches is that the flap is reinforced and thicker than the rest of the sock, thus creating cushioning and better resistance to wear in a shoe with a back. The heel stitch pattern used in the *Simply Splendid Socks* is slightly altered from the regular method (it may take the hardened sock knitter a while to adapt!), as the slipped stitches are on the wrong side rows rather than the more customary right side rows. This is somewhat more efficient as the needle needs to enter each stitch of the row from the same purlwise direction. It also reduces the possibility of accidentally twisted slipped stitches when alternating between knit stitches and stitches slipped purlwise.

The length of the heel flap is very important. The more rows in the flap, the greater the number of stitches that will be knitted up along either side, giving greater depth to the sock. This creates a larger turning space to permit the foot and ankle to enter the sock. The rule of thumb is to knit the flap as long as it is wide; if the flap is too short the sock will be difficult to put on and will have a tendency to slip down and under the heel as you walk. For those with high insteps, a slightly longer flap is better suited; for those with flatter insteps, slightly shorter than square is best. Check the fit of the ankle and adjust your future flap lengths accordingly.

✓ To test the squareness of the heel flap, at the end of a heel flap row, fold the flap diagonally. If the needle lies parallel to the side of the flap with no extra heel flap showing, you have a square. Keep going — don't skimp on it.

Turning the Heel

In turning the heel, again we can adjust the resulting heel shape and the number of stitches remaining after the turn. For an average sock, make the decrease positions at the two-third and one-third positions across the flap. This gives a pleasantly rounded, well-fitting heel. For those with narrower feet, you may wish to make the first short row at three-fifths and two-fifths across. The more short rows, the more decreases and fewer remaining sole stitches. The nearer to the mid-point of the flap you make the first short row, the more V-shaped (rather than U-shaped) the heel will be.

✓ The short rows for turning the Common Heel are worked in plain stocking stitch. This is a thin fabric, for one of the areas of heaviest wear in the whole sock. Make it more durable by adding a reinforcing yarn (woolly nylon or fine mohair) to your working yarn or by weaving in another yarn at the back of the work or by using two yarns in an alternating "salt and pepper" pattern. (Use both ends of the same ball for single colour socks.) The toe may be reinforced similarly.

Instep Decreases

The number of stitches on the needles after the heel is turned is controlled by the depth of the heel flap and the number of sole stitches remaining. If you should have an extra rogue stitch on one side or other of the heel flap, surreptitiously decrease this away on the first round at the junction of the sole. From the new much-larger number of stitches, the aim is to taper the sock back to the original number we started with, which is perfect if the foot has the same circumference as the ankle. This is a good time to check the lower foot measurement. Is it significantly different from the ankle measurement? If so, calculate the ideal number of total stitches for you (gauge x foot circumference).

The rate of decrease is adjustable. For fine yarn socks, a decrease on either side of the instep every round works well, but with "chubby" yarn, every alternate round may be better. It is possible to adjust the rate of decrease to suit the silhouette of the foot. For example, begin by decreasing every round and taper to every alternate or every third round if desired. Continue to make decreases until the desired number of stitches is obtained.

✓ For peace of mind and fine fit, you can try the sock on at any stage. Slip the stitches onto a length of yarn and pop it on.

Eccentric Toes

Toe shaping is a highly personal issue. Begin thinking about the toes as soon as your sock reaches the base of the little toe. Shape with whatever frequency you feel best suits the shape of the foot. A toe can be shaped at different rates at either side to give it a customized fit. Although the idea of customizing the toe shaping is very appealing, it has certain drawbacks. You have to be very alert in the mornings to be able to put the socks on the correct feet, and more seriously, the wear points for each sock will never change, possibly resulting in holes sooner rather than later. There are many alternative toes, as there are heels and cuffs. Experiment with working your way, toe by toe, until you find your favourite.

Long Leg Calculations

Careful measurements need to be taken to achieve a shapely, tailored leg. Extra measurements are needed for a knee-high sock.

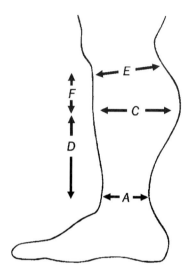

Diagram 12.
A-Ankle; C-Calf-maximum; D-Lower shin;
E-Under knee; F-Upper shin.

Using your stitch gauge, you can establish the number of stitches needed at the ankle, calf-maximum and under-knee.

Round all stitch numbers to an even number. By calculating the difference in stitch numbers at the various positions, the number of pairs of increases or decreases can be determined. (Divide the difference by two.)

Using your row gauge, you can determine the number of rounds between these positions.

SOCK FIT AND ADJUSTMENT

By dividing the number of rounds by the number of pairs of increases/decreases, the shaping frequency for each leg section can be determined.

For example:

For a gauge of 9 sts x 12 rows = 1 square inch
Measurements:

A = 10", E = 14", C = 15", F = 4", D = 8"

At the **A**nkle (10 x 9) = 90 stitches will be needed.

At Calf maximum C, (8 x 12) = 96 rows higher, (15 x 9) = 135 stitches will be required.

Round down to 134 stitches.

The difference is 44 stitches or 22 pairs of increases, 96/22 = 4.36 (approximately 4).

Therefore make pairs of increases every fourth round until 134 stitches are reached.

At **E** under knee, (4 x 12) = 48 rows higher, (14 x 9) = 126 stitches will be required.

The difference is 8 stitches or 4 pairs of decreases, 48/4 = 12.

Therefore make pairs of decreases every twelfth round until 126 stitches are reached.

Increases are usually made at the back of the sock as this is where the calf muscle waxes and wanes. Increases can be placed between the first and second stitches, and the penultimate and last stitches of the round. This gives an elegant double column of stitches down the centre back.

An alternative approach to leg shaping can be taken by adjusting needle sizes. The leg doesn't need to be knit as firmly as the foot. The same calculations can be made based on a slightly looser "leg gauge," but using the "foot gauge" to determine the number of stitches at the ankle.

For a less precise, but more spontaneous leg, increase the needle size every couple of inches up the leg until the height of the maximum calf measurement is reached. From this point, reduce the needle size again (at a faster rate). The leg up to the maximum may involve four different increasing needle sizes, and above this point only two decreasing sizes, as the leg is larger below the knee than at the ankle.

A fold-over cuff or a knitted-in facing at the top of a knee sock is very useful to avoid constricting the leg. It adds extra support to hold the sock up and can be used to hide a garter! I-cord worked in an elastic yarn makes excellent garters. Another approach is to determine the maximum calf measurement and cast on an appropriate number of stitches, but work a good length of

2 x 2 rib to tailor the shape above the calf before changing to stocking stitch.

Working upward from the ankle offers much liberation when fitting the leg of a sock. It allows you to test the leg periodically. If wishing to work a top-down foot and an ankle-up leg, begin at the ankle with a Provisional Crochet Cast-On (see page 110) and later return to this edge to complete the sock.

There is a common misconception that when working in the opposite direction from an existing piece of knitting, the knitting will be different in some respect, that perhaps it will rotate in a different direction or appear inside out. However, it will feel and look no different to the knitter. The only point of significance is that the new-direction stitches will be half-a-stitch out of alignment with the old-direction stitches. This is imperceptible in single-yarn stocking stitch. We are working into the valleys between the original stitches. For more detail see "What is Going On" page 112. Only patterns with vertical alignment would be affected, such as ribs and two-colour-per-round patterns. For this reason, make a direction change before or after a section of ribbing and at a break between colour patterns. The tail of the yarn from the old direction will need to be unthreaded from the first of the new loops.

When changing the direction of the work with a self-patterning yarn, attention may need to be paid to the directionality of the yarn!

Sock Finishing

Sock finishing is fairly minimal, but it's worth being particular about. Grafting either the toe or the heel, neatening any ends, gathering closed any little holes and duplicating any stressed stitches are all usually involved.

Grafting or Kitchener Stitch

This is a seamless way to connect opposing live stitches. It usually occurs at the toe or heel of a sock. See page 117, for an alternative and superior method of grafting.

Neatening Yarn Tails

Leave long tails when adding in new yarns. Joins are potential weak spots in a sock and the yarn should be darned in further than is usual. Any Superwash treatment of the yarn (which allows you to take liberties when washing), will mean that yarn tails will not bed themselves into place quickly. If possible, make any necessary joins in the sole. Later, darn the tails in with a sharp needle on the diagonal in a zig-zag path, grazing the plies of the yarn inside the sock. Subsequent tails can be zag-zigged to cross and lock in the first tail. Weaving the tails into the sole adds to the thickness and warmth.

Closing the Gaps

Use the Circular Suture method (see page 115) to close any gaps at sides of Turkish Heels or instep. Duplicate Stitch (see page 115) any stretched stitches, either internally or externally, with matching yarn (this is where odd pieces of yarn may come in handy for a colour match). Use the tail(s) left from casting on to tidy any small gap in the initial edge.

Blocking

For the most pristine finish, block the sock. The simplest method of blocking is to put the sock onto a willing foot (give the owner a good book, chocolate, some knitting or any combination of the three), and then lightly mist the sock with a cold water spray, pat the moisture into the sock and leave it to dry. Alternatively, both flat and three-dimensional sock blockers are available. This treatment will make a huge difference to stranded fabrics such as with the *Chequerboard Socks,* helping to remove the slight wrinkles caused by the floats or weaving.

Washing

Wash according to the yarn manufacturer's directions. Hand wash if possible. Machine washing is cruel. Even though it may not destroy the sock, it may well fluff it considerably and generally assist premature aging. (Of the sock rather than the knitter.) It is a reassuring thought, though, that if the sock ever stowed away up the leg of a pair of trousers, it would come through the ordeal without shrinkage. To speed the drying of hand-washed socks, spin them in a salad spinner before laying them flat to dry.

Wearing and Display

Wear your socks with pride. Many knitters select their footwear to complement or reveal their socks. Transparent footwear both in ankle boot and clog form is available. Open sandals are also popular.

Single socks make an eye-catching textile arrangement if mounted on cardboard forms.

Double-Pointed Needle Techniques

Getting started on rigid or flexible double-pointed needles and tips for achieving an even fabric

Like bicycling, the trickiest part of working in small circles is getting started.

Casting On onto Rigid Double-Pointed Needles

Method 1 - With cast on stitches divided into two sections.

1. Cast on all the required stitches onto a single dpn.
2. Place a second needle tip-to-tip with the first and divide the stitches evenly onto the two needles.
3. Fold the two needles parallel to each other, keeping the needle with the first stitch cast on at the front of the work. Slide the front needle to the left, so the first stitch cast on is near the tip.
4. Check that the cast on edge lies underneath both needles without twists.
   The twists are caused by the cast on edge snaking unbidden around the needle(s). This may occur in round knitting of any size, particularly on overcrowded needles. If you do not

spot this problem, you can eventually find yourself knitting merrily away on a Möbius strip, which while it has its uses, makes for a poor sock or sweater. Check as directed at the beginning of the first round. Make an extra check at the beginning of the second round, too. If a twist is discovered at this point, it can be moved around the edge so that it falls into the single strand of yarn linking the round. To check for twists, try placing the cast-on edge on a table top while you run your eye around the edge.

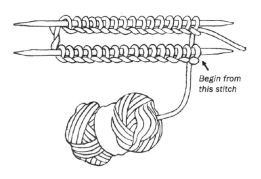

Begin from
this stitch

Diagram 13 shows Method 1, Step 3.

5. With a third needle, work the first quarter of the stitches, using the yarn leading from the last stitch cast on.

6. With a fourth needle, work the remainder of the stitches from the front needle (second quarter of the stitches). There are now three needles in your work.

7. Using the fourth needle, work the next quarter of the stitches.

8. With your final needle, work the last quarter of the stitches. The round should be joined by one strand, linking the last stitch to the first.

9. Take the empty needle and work the first quarter of the stitches again to start the second round.

When the first round is worked by Method 1, it can feel awkward to work the first few stitches because the needles are so close together. This is compensated for by the reduced number of needles you are handling initially.

Why not cast on onto four separate needles straight away? This is quite possible and acceptable. However, the edge can be difficult to manage and can easily become distorted between needles. There is also a greater possibility of a twist sneaking into the edge.

Method 2 - With cast on stitches divided into three sections.

If you do not like the above method, here is another way!

1. Cast onto a single needle.

2. Divide the stitches into three groups by slipping one-third of the stitches onto a second needle and one-third onto a third needle (similar to Step 2 in Method 1).

3. Fold the stitches into a triangle, keeping the needle with the first stitch cast on at the front. Hold the triangle steady. Triangles are delightfully stable.

4. Check the cast-on edge for twists. *See Step 4 in Method 1.*

5. Begin work from the first stitch cast on, using the yarn leading from the last stitch cast on. Your stitches are on 3 needles and you are working with a fourth needle.

6. Introduce a fourth stitch-holding needle at your convenience.

To introduce a fourth stitch-holding needle, place a beginning/end marker if necessary (*see page 113*); work approximately three quarters of the stitches from Needle #1 onto an empty needle, work the remaining quarter of the stitches from Needle #1 and half of those from Needle #2 onto the next needle, work the remaining half from Needle #2 and a quarter from Needle #3 onto another. By this time you will have four needles in the work and similar numbers of stitches on each needle. Fine-tune the positioning of the stitches to suit your taste or to fit the dictates of the stitch pattern. Your stitches will now be on four needles and you are working with a fifth needle.

Where to Put the New Needle?

When knitting, put the needle into the new stitch in front, and to the left of, the old needle.

When purling, put the needle into the new stitch from the right and behind the old needle.

These needle positions are only suggestions. The many different ways of holding the needles can affect the best way to enter the next stitch. I find it easiest to hold the right-hand needle from below (like a chopstick) for the first few stitches. This gives initial support to the needle. Then I return to my more customary hand position above the needles for the remainder of the needle, and hold the left-hand needle from above.

Getting Started on Flexible Double-Pointed Needles — Circular

If you really find that you don't enjoy circular knitting on rigid dpns, try this circular technique.

The First Round

1. Cast on all the required stitches onto a single circular needle. Length is largely immaterial (use a 40 cm/16" to avoid excessive dangling needle length).

2. Place a second needle tip-to-tip with the first and divide the stitches evenly onto the two needles. Two needles are the minimum, described here, but more may be used if you wish.

3. Fold the two needles parallel to each other, placing the needle with the first stitch cast on at the front.

4. Check that the cast on edge lies underneath both needles without twists. *(See Step 4 in Method 1.)*

5. Slide the needle with the first stitches cast on, to the left such that the first stitch cast on is near the needle-tip. With the opposite end

of the SAME needle and the yarn leading from the last stitch cast on, work all of the stitches on this needle. Slide the stitches to the middle of the needle.

6. Turn the work to the beginning of the other needle and slide the needle to the left through the stitches so that the next stitch to be worked is near the needle tip. With the opposite end of the SAME needle and the yarn leading from the last stich worked, work all of the stitches on this needle. Slide the stitches to the middle of the needle.

From this point onwards continue always to work the stitches on a particular needle with the opposite end of the SAME needle.

A sock may be knit using either rigid or flexible needles. Patterns may be written a little differently, assuming a certain needle type, but there is no reason that the other type of needle cannot be used. More than two flexible needles may also be used.

Sock Techniques

While this book is not intended to be a comprehensive manual of knitting techniques, the methods described are favourites of mine and are used in the various sock patterns. If they are new to you, they are worth the investment of a little time to experiment with. With your favourite needles in hand, and regular-sized practice yarn standing by, read the directions and give them a whirl on just a few stitches. Many of these methods are not solely useful for socks and may add a little panache to other areas of your knitting life.

Yarn Butterflies

Lengths of yarn that would otherwise tangle or un-ply can be kept tidy and controllable by making a yarn butterfuly. They also dispense easily from the end from which the winding began. (*See page 107.*)

To wind a butterfly, pinch the start of the yarn between the thumb and middle finger of the left hand with the yarn leading up toward the index finger. Hold your index finger two inches apart from the middle finger and wind the yarn around the index and tip of middle finger a number of times. The yarn may be wound in a figure of eight manner if desired. Keep the butterfly fairly small when you first practice.

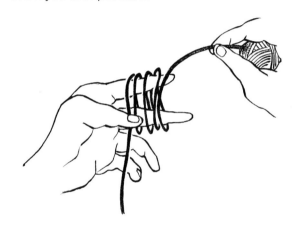

Diagram 14.

Slip the bundle of yarn carefully off your fingers and wind the yarn *firmly* around the middle of the bundle at least five times.

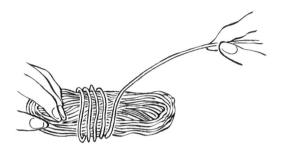

Diagram 15.

After the final turn, secure with a half-hitch.

To make the hitch, place the index and middle finger of your right hand above the yarn leading to the ball with the thumb below and pinch the yarn; now twist your hand to the right, and tip both fingers upwards through the resulting loop. Part the fingers to enlarge the loop and, with the left hand, tuck the butterfly halfway up into the loop between the fingers. See *Diagram 16.*

Tighten up the hitch and cut off the yarn, leaving only a short tail. Test the butterfly. It should pull out from the end that you originally held when winding.

Caution, be on the lookout for reversed hitches! Faulty hitches resemble a U with the yarn tail protruding through it. These hitches can come undone without your permission. Practice the hitch until you become proficient.

Should the knack of the hitch elude you: make the turns around the middle of the butterfly as usual, cut the yarn off from the ball with a 15 cm/6" tail remaining, make a final turn over your finger and then tuck yarn tail under this loose turn and tighten. Cut off any surplus tail.

Diagram 16.

Long Tail (Continental) Cast-On

If you were to learn only one cast-on method, this would be the one I'd recommend. It forms an excellent general-purpose edge. It is known by a variety of names and it forms the basis of many other more elaborate cast on edges, which become easier to follow once this one is mastered.

You will need working yarn and a single needle.

Two Handed Method

Unwind a tail of yarn approximately four times the intended cast-on edge length. Make a slip knot. Place the slip knot onto a needle and firm up the loop to gently fit the needle. Place the ball of working yarn out to your right.

*Hold the tail yarn out to the left with your left thumb above it. Make a loop in the yarn by dropping the tip of the thumb in a circular motion, first down away from you, back towards you and then up to its original position. There should now be a loop of yarn around the thumb (as it crosses the thumb it should look like the middle portion of an S).

Slide the tip of the needle (holding the slip knot) up the side of the thumb into the loop. Leave the thumb in the loop.

With the right hand, throw the yarn leading to the ball around the needle as if to knit.

With the left thumb push the loop up and over the needle-tip and extricate the thumb.

While maintaining a gentle tension on the working yarn leading to the ball, tighten the tail yarn. The yarn thrown around the needle should now look like a stitch.

You should feel a little resistance as the loop firms up underneath the needle.

Repeat from * for each stitch. The slipknot is also counted as a stitch.

One Handed Method

This method of casting on may also be worked holding both yarn and tail in one hand, without the initial slip knot. With the tail to the left and ball to the right, put the thumb and first finger of the left hand under the yarn, with finger tips toward you. Hold the tail yarn down with the third and fourth fingers and the working yarn with the middle finger.

With the right hand, put the needle tip under the yarn between thumb and index finger; let the right index finger rest on the yarn and needle where the yarn touches the needle. *Take the needle tip over to the left and back under the outside strand, then over across to the right and back under the inside strand. Bring the needle across to the left, between the strands forming a loop on the thumb and let the loop drop off the thumb to the right of the needle. Firm up the loop.

Worked in this fashion, two stitches will be created on the first occasion only. Thereafter repeat from * to create individual new stitches.

What is going on?

The new stitches are formed by the working yarn (held on the right, leading to the ball) being thrown around the needle just as in regular knitting. These stitches form an edge because they are each being held by a loop of tail yarn around the base. The tension on the right-hand yarn controls the firmness of the new stitches; keep this gentle but firm, similar to your usual knitting tension. If your cast-on stitches are habitually too tight, then practice relaxing the tension on this yarn as you cast on. The newly cast-on stitches should be only fractionally more difficult to work than your regular mid-project stitches.

The spacing of the stitches is controlled by the tail yarn (held to the left). The elasticity of the edge is directly linked to how closely the stitches are placed together on the needle. For socks, maximum edge elasticity is required to permit the sock to stretch around the heel. With practice it is possible to space the new stitches farther apart than might be usual. The secret to controlling the spacing is to keep the left-hand yarn at 90 degrees or less away from the needle (measured from the tip). As you tighten the left-hand yarn, do not allow the stitch to slide very close to the preceding stitch.

After counting and checking your cast-on edge, cut off all but 6" of any remaining yarn tail left over from casting on. (To find a knitter who has never launched forth on their knitting only to find that they were working with the tail yarn, would be an Herculean task!)

Other than for tubular cast on, don't use a larger-than-gauge needle size for regular casting on. This only creates elongated stitches but no extra distance between the adjacent stitches. The resulting edge is slightly looser, but only because everything is a little sloppy.

Refinements

To add extra elasticity and strength to this edge try doubling the tail yarn.

When working very long edges, the long tail tends to drag on the ground and it may become un-plied and therefore weakened by the twisting action of the left-hand loops. To avoid this, wind the tail into a yarn butterfly *(see page 104)* that will dispense from the cast-on position. The yarn will then be able to dangle freely as you cast on and any excess twist can be dissipated by the free turning of the butterfly.

Channel Island Cast-On

What appears to hold the Channel Island Cast-On back from widespread popularity is that it takes a little practice to achieve an even edge, and it feels quite uncontrollable in the initial stages. Please don't let this deter you. Even some notably excellent reference works cunningly gloss over the nitty gritty about how to get started!

These minor problems are easily surmounted by a determined knitter with an eye on a gem, take a look at the photograph on page 21.

Practice with a plain wool yarn on a single light-weight, matte, medium size, straight needle.

1. Measure a tail of yarn six times as long as the intended cast on. Double the tail up to form a loop three times the intended length of the cast-on. Lay the ball to your right and the loop extending to the left.

2. Hold your left hand palm downwards. With the right hand, take hold of the doubled yarn near the tail, lift up the open end of the loop between the thumb and first finger of the left hand. The loop dangles below from the crook between the thumb and first finger. See Diagram 17.

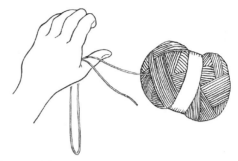

Diagram 17.

3. Lead the tail, and the yarn attached to the ball, out to the right. With the right hand, wrap the double yarn gently around the left thumb counterclockwise (looking down on the top of the thumb). Pull extra yarn through from the loop if necessary. See Diagram 18. Press the tail of the yarn against the side of the left thumb with the left index finger. Let go of the yarn with the right hand.

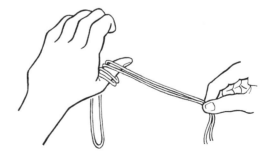

Diagram 18.

4. Slide the needle along the right-hand side of the left thumb between the thumb and all four strands of yarn. *See Diagram 19.* Keep the needle above the finger that is securing the tail. Support the needle against your body in this position. With the right hand and the yarn attached to the ball only, throw the yarn knitwise around the tip of the needle. With the needle, draw the thrown yarn through both of the double thumb loops, to create a stitch. Stabilize the stitch and the double loops against the needle with the right index finger and thumb. Gently extract your left thumb.

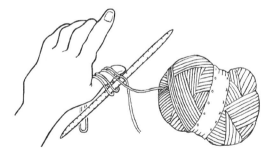

Diagram 19.

5. Keep your right index finger in place on the stitch. Gently pull the slack out of the thumb loops by pulling on the main loop with the left hand. One very delicate stitch is now on the needle.

6. Now stabilize this stitch with your left hand and make a "yarn over" with the working yarn (throw as if to knit). This forms the second stitch. Do not allow the stitches to twist around the needle; secure them with your right hand.

7. Double-wrap your thumb as before and repeat from #4. When tightening the subsequent thumb loops, ensure that you bring the stitch up adjacent to its neighbor. Stitches are formed in pairs; a knitted double wrap followed by a yarn over.

8. Be very careful not to lose the final stitch, made only with an over. Twisting the yarn tails together or making a temporary knot after casting on the last stitch is helpful.

9. If the stitches have been cast on in pairs, the first row or round will always commence with a knit stitch. The first round (or second row) is the right side of this cast-on edge. The knits will line up with the lumps produced by the double overs and the purls with the gully between when viewed from the right side.

Watch out for skipped "yarn over" stitches — they are so simple that it is easy to overlook them.

When casting on for a sock, work onto a single needle, secure the final stitch with a temporary knot and then divide the stitches between your needles. There will be three tails to darn in when neatening the sock top.

Provisional Crochet Cast-On

This is an exceedingly useful temporary method for beginning a piece of knitting when live loops (to be used as stitches) are *definitely* going to be required at this edge at a later stage of the work. The temporary or provisional stitches are created with a brightly contrasting waste yarn, to avoid confusion the waste yarn should be of a similar weight to prevent distortion of the stitches. This edge is easily unravelled whenever the live loops are required.

You will need contrasting, similar-weight WY, a crochet hook and a single double-pointed needle. Make a slip knot near the beginning of the WY. *Put the crochet hook through the slip-knot loop. Place the needle on top of the yarn leading to the ball, *put the hook over the needle and catch the yarn with the hook and bring the yarn through, creating a new loop on the crochet hook and also one provisional stitch on the needle. Take the working yarn around the needle-tip and back underneath the needle; repeat from * until the required number of provisional stitches have been made on the needle. *See Diagram 20.* Finish with a few extra chain stitches off the needle. Manipulate as before, but without throwing the yarn around the needle. This creates a short chain to indicate that this is the end to unravel from later. Cut the WY and pull the tail through the final loop to secure it.

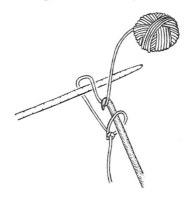

Diagram 20.

What is going on?

If you were to slip the provisional stitches off your needle, you would see that you have created a crochet chain. A crochet chain will unravel easily, provided none of the sides of the chain are caught and the final stitch is live. This method places the back of the crochet chain around the needle between each chain stitch and ensures that the chain will unravel easily on every occasion.

Refinements and Other Uses

When using this method for a large number of stitches, add a couple of extra stitches onto the needle before making the final chain. Make a final accurate count of the number of stitches and slip off any extras at the chain end. This is easier than having to add a few extras if your first estimate of the stitch number was off.

A similar result is achieved by knitting up stitches into each of the "backs" (the length of yarn between each chain stitch) of an independently-worked, loose crochet chain. However, identifying the "back" of the chain with absolute accuracy along an entire edge is not always easy, often resulting in having to cut out sections of the temporary edge.

This edge, if worked in the main colour, may also be used as a permanent edge. It is then called the "Cast-Off" cast on, as the resulting edge matches a conventional bound-off edge. This is useful for projects where the cast-on and bind-off edges are both visible to the public, as in the case of scarves and table runners. Just as with regular bound-off edges, however, this cast on is not highly elastic, and is not suited to socks!

For a permanent edge, work this cast on exactly as previously given, using the working yarn; the final stitch is formed by taking the last loop on the crochet hook and placing it onto the needle.

Check the resulting edge for twisted stitches in the chain edge. If you have twists (and if you care!), these can be prevented by either removing your hook from each resulting loop and replacing your hook into the loop from the opposite direction, or altering the direction from which you hook your yarn. This detail is only of aesthetic importance and makes no difference to the effectiveness of the provisional or permanent edge.

Tubular Cast-On

A tubular cast on makes a soft, elastic, rounded edge, with a small channel between the layers of fabric. It may be used for both 1 x 1 and 2 x 2 ribbed edges. There is a great deal of unnecessary myth and magic surrounding this cast on, and several methods of achieving it. This one is straightforward and controllable.

Method

Onto a single double-pointed needle at *least* 3 sizes larger than you wish to use for the sock, using the PCCO method, with WY of a strongly contrasting colour cast on half of the required number of stitches (this must be an even number for a 2 x 2 rib).

Beginning at the unravellable end of the provisional cast-on edge, with the Main sock yarn and larger needles, establish knitting in the round, adding in the extra needles at each approximate quarter point.

Knit three rounds of Main sock yarn. The resulting stitches will be quite loose. Now follow the directions for your chosen rib type.

For 1 x 1 rib: With *regular* needle size, [k1, yfw between needles (ready to purl), with the right-hand needle lift the Main yarn float (between the first two provisional stitches), and purl into it] repeat to last stitch, end k1, place the Main yarn tail over left-hand needle from back to front and under the needle to the back again; hold it so. Purl into the resulting O. This scraggy stitch will neaten beautifully later, using the tail. Continue to work in 1 x 1 rib as now established.

For 2 x 2 rib: With *regular* needle size, [k1, yfw between needles (ready to purl), with right-hand needle lift the Main yarn float (between the first two provisional stitches), and purl into it. With the right-hand needle, lift the next Main yarn float and purl into it, k1 (four stitches are now on right-hand needle: k, p, p, k)] repeat to last

stitch. The final float is a little vague, so pick the most promising strand of Main yarn!

What is going on?

This rolled edge is formed by using "stitches" from both the top and bottom edges of a thin strip of stocking stitch fabric. By folding the strip of knit fabric up, the stitches from the upper edge of the knitting can be alternated with the loops (between the stitches) from the initial edge, thus almost doubling the number of stitches originally cast on.

Think of the structure of a single row (or round) of knitting once it is off the needles.

Four knit stitches
Three valley stitches

Diagram 21.

It is an undulating strand of yarn, comprised of a series of hills and valleys. The hills we recognise as stitches. If we were to turn the picture upside down, the valleys could also be considered to be stitches.

Note that the valley stitches are half a stitch out of alignment with the hill stitches. With flat knitting, there is always one less valley stitch than hill stitches (as they lie between two hills). In round knitting there are equal numbers.

When using the Provisional Crochet Cast-On, the dips of the valley stitches show through between each provisional chain stitch.

In conventional cast-on methods we secure the valleys (the left-hand yarn does this in Continental Cast-On), so that the loops cannot ladder. However, if the loops were left unsecured, or later released, it would be possible to knit from them.

To achieve a particular number of stitches with this edge, PCCO half of the required number of stitches. Considerably larger needles are used to give the rows with only half of the number of stitches sufficient elasticity and length to comfortably stretch around a row (or round) with double the number of gauge-size stitches.

Once the stocking stitch section is complete, the resulting fabric is folded up behind the stitches on the needle. Then the stitches are worked alternately: knit one upper stitch, purl one lower valley stitch.

Why are the lower valley stitches purled? Because as the flap of fabric is folded up behind the stitches on the needle, the valley loops present themselves as purl stitches (you are looking at the opposite side of the fabric). Happily, this sets up a perfect 1 x 1 rib if the stitches are alternated.

To create a 2 x 2 rib, swap the order of every third and fourth stitch; k p k p k p k p becomes k p p k k p p k. To do this, after working the first pair as usual, purl the second valley loop before knitting the next stitch from the needle. It's as simple as that — not magic but sleight of hand!

Running Yarn Marker

This form of marker is particularly useful when working in the round on a set of needles, as it will not drop off if it happens to lie at a junction between two needles. Markers may be used to indicate the beginning and end point of the round, or the width of a pattern repeat or as a reminder to make decreases.

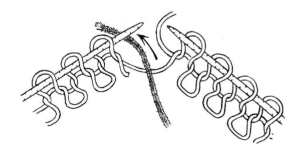

Diagram 22 shows how to place a Running Yarn Marker.

Method

A running marker is a short length of contrasting yarn placed between the needles at the appropriate position. (If you throw with your left hand, ensure that the marker yarn is placed underneath the working yarn.) As you work the next stitch, the yarn is trapped in position underneath a single strand of working yarn. *See Diagram 22.* On each successive round, flip the upper end of the marker yarn in the opposite direction. This leaves a line of marker yarn up the work; it may be pulled up the work as you go or removed when no longer required.

Refinements

The yarn chosen for the marker should, for clarity, contrast with the working yarn and be fairly fine in weight. A fat yarn would cause distortion between the two adjacent stitches. A smooth yarn such as mercerized cotton is fine but it requires more flips to anchor it in the work. Fluffy yarns are less likely to slide out unbidden, but beware of glaring rogue fibers shed into your work! Begin with an 8" length of marker yarn. It is very easy to sit on longer pieces and then accidentally pull them out of the knitting as you lift your work to knit. If you wish to leave the marker in place for later reference, simply tie on extra lengths of marker yarn as needed; if not, keep

pulling the top end of the marker up the work as you advance. Should the marker disappear in a puff of green smoke, or be pulled out, it can be reinserted using a blunt darning needle.

Colour-coded markers can also be helpful. Use a different colour for the beginning of the round and other colours to demarcate the side positions, pattern repeats or decreases.

Once the marker yarn is reasonably secure in the work, *i.e.* when it has been anchored several times, there is no need to flip it every round. Every few rounds is sufficient. Markers can be used in this manner to assist in measuring the frequency of short rows, cable repeats and shapings, by flipping the adjacent marker only on the appropriate rounds.

Darning and Sutures

Little gaps are a fact of life with socks. There are several places where we manipulate a stitch just beyond what we can reasonably expect it to happily tolerate; for example, at the junction between the heel flap and the instep stitches or at the sides of the Turkish Heel. There seem to be two schools of thought on the subject of holes — those who knit into them and decrease away the extra stitches and those who employ a little cunning stitchery. Use the knitting-into method with caution. It can leave a permanent boggle in the sock, emphasizing rather than disguising the problem. Once a hole has been knitted closed, the only way to later remove the boggle is to unpick back to it.

The sewn methods are usually the last detail in the finishing process. If you are not happy with the result of the stitching, the sewing yarn can easily be removed and reworked by another method.

Circular Suture

Worked from the inside of the sock with a sharp needle and matching yarn, this is a quick and easy way of gathering a hole and closing it. With a short length of yarn, sew once around the circumference of the hole, splitting the plies of the sock yarn with the sharp needle.

Draw the circle of yarn closed and take the sewing needle through the darning yarn where it began the circle, to lock it together. Finish by taking the darning yarn across the diameter of the circle, splitting the plies on both sides.

If using this method where it might one day need to be undone, for example on a Turkish Heel that might be replaced should it ever wear out, make the sutures in a slightly different colour so they may be located and easily removed.

Duplicate Stitches

These are exactly as the name implies, a straightforward sewn duplication of the stitches of the knitted fabric. There will be odd stitches that, no matter how you darn or suture behind the scenes, still look over-stretched and distorted. The stitches that anchor the sides of the Garter Stitch Short Row heel, for example, are carrying a heavy load. While it is unlikely that they will ever break, they will look better if you duplicate stitch over them.

Take a length of matching yarn and a blunt darning needle and, from the right side of the work, follow the path of the yarn around the stretched stitch. According to the amount of distortion it may be even better to duplicate the neighbouring stitches as well. Once you are happy with the appearance of the stitch, take the tails of yarn through to the back of the work, adjust the stitch and darn and neaten the tails.

Waste Yarn Openings

If you will later need an opening in a knitted fabric, with live loops on both edges for use as stitches, this method is very easy and secure. This technique is often used for mitten thumbs and pockets, and in this book for the Turkish Heel.

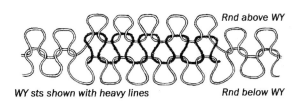

WY sts shown with heavy lines

Rnd above WY

Rnd below WY

Diagram 23.

Method

Knit as usual to the planned opening position, let go of the Main working yarn and allow it to dangle. Take a length of WY, brightly contrasting to the Main yarn to avoid confusion, and of a similar weight to prevent distortion of the stitches. Knit across the required number of stitches for the opening, leaving a tail of WY at both ends to prevent these stitches from coming undone. Slip the WY stitches back onto the left-hand needle to bring you back to the working yarn. (Slipping is not always necessary when working on dpns if the first WY stitch is at the beginning of a needle.) With the Main yarn, resume knitting across the WY stitches and onwards.

When the opening is required you may either remove the WY and slip the resulting loops onto temporary needles or, if this is more than your heart can take, slide a fine needle under the right-hand side of each of the original stitches

(marked X), turn the work upside down and repeat for the loops on the far side of the WY (marked O) before removing the WY.

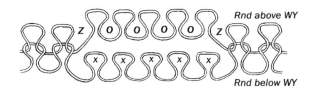

Rnd above WY

Rnd below WY

Diagram 24.

It is not strictly necessary to pick up the ambiguous partial loops (marked Z); they are quite secure whether you pick them up or not. There will be one less loop on the far side of the opening than there were WY stitches worked, so it is common practice to pick up one of the ambiguous loops to make the numbers equal on both sides. If you choose to pick up both, decrease one of them away on your first round thereafter.

Refinements

When working into the WY stitches of a two-colour-per-round pattern, carry one of the yarns at the back of the work. Otherwise you will be trying to find loops comprised of two pieces of yarn. The slight interruption to the pattern will be disguised as part of the heel when it is knitted.

Be certain that you really do want the opening and that the positioning is correct, as once the WY is set in it will take some effort and skilled grafting to conceal the hole.

Grafting with a Toe Chimney

The grafting of sock toes, also called the Kitchener Stitch, has caused many a knitter to gnash their teeth! Tiny stitches and dark multi ply yarns contribute to the difficulties, but grafting really isn't hard. I take a slightly different approach from the customary graft-it-off-the-needles method, it offers a couple of hidden bonuses, even to the contented off-the-needle grafter. I see little value in filling my precious mental hard-drive with formulas and mantras, so this method is a self-illustrated version, involving no vulnerable live stitches.

Complete the knitting at the side of the sock. You will have 16-20 stitches awaiting humane disposal. With brightly contrasting WY of a similar weight, work circularly on these remaining stitches, producing a little tube; about six rounds is sufficient. The tube should be long enough for you to hold inside the sock. Slip these stitches onto the tail of the WY or bind them off.

The photograph above illustrates the toe of the sock with its temporary WY chimney.

Take a fine, blunt needle (a tapestry needle is ideal) threaded with a 15" length of unattached sock yarn. Tuck the tube of WY inside the sock and hold it from within the sock with your non-sewing hand. Manipulate the tube to approximately match the mid-points.

Sewing begins in the middle of the toe. Find two sock stitches side by side at the mid-point of one side of the toe. With your needle, *follow the path of the WY as it intersects with the sock stitches on either side.* If you pinch the entering and exiting strands of the grafting yarn together, from the direction of the opening, it should resemble a regular knit stitch interlocked with another regular stitch.

If the connected sock stitch looks more like parallel lines ||, *you have gone behind a whole sock stitch, not through the loops of two different ones. Remove the yarn and try again.*

FOLLOW THE WY EXACTLY.

Pull only half of the grafting yarn through this first stitch. Leave the remaining half for sewing in the other direction.

Bring your needle to the opposite side of the toe, and repeat with another pair of adjacent sock stitches immediately opposite the first pair. Always keep the needle pointing in the same direction (toward the side of the toe you are heading for). Check this newly sewn stitch also.

From this point on, take your needle across to the opposite fabric and into the sock stitch last exited, and follow the WY out through the neighbouring stitch. Repeat.

Do not pull the grafting yarn tight. The grafted stitches should be the same size and shape as your regular stitches.

The graft is completed (as far as is possible) when one strand of grafting yarn has gone through each of the two side stitches. Leave the remaining tail of yarn dangling and resume sewing from the mid-point with the length of yarn left ready. You may find it easiest to turn the

sock through 180 degrees and sew in the same direction as before.

The photograph above illustrates the sock toe, viewed from above, with WY tucked inside.

The fiddliest stitches are at the edges. Stuff your fingers up underneath to check that all stitches are secure. There should be two pieces of grafting yarn through each stitch (resembling an unbroken knitted fabric), apart from the outer two stitches on each side. Once you are happy with the graft, rip out the WY.

Now decide where to pull the grafting threads through to the inside of the sock, so as to best tidy any tatty stitches at the extremities. It is better to use the separate piece of yarn for grafting, rather than the tail left over from the knitting, as you will have a tail on either side of the toe which which to tidy the piggy stitches.

Three-Needle Bind-Off

Here is a very useful method of simultaneously binding off and joining two edges. Although not ideal for sock toes, it can be used when desperate. It also works for the miniature socks. With wrong sides together, this makes an adequate join for the Turkish heel, as the seam is then external and not likely to cause any discomfort.

This technique is also ideally suited to many shoulder seams; it is quick and neat and provides the necessary reinforcement to prevent shoulders stretching due to the weight of the sleeves.

Preparation

You have two equal sets of stitches to be bound off together, each on its own needle, preferably double-pointed. Place the pieces right sides together (for an internal seam), with their respective needles parallel to each other.

Picture shows a sock toe, wrong side out, ready to begin a three needle bind-off.

Method

Beginning at the edge with yarn attached, *insert the tip of a third knitting needle of a similar size into the first stitch on each needle, as if to knit. With matching yarn, knit the two stitches together onto the right-hand needle. Repeat from *. Now you have 2 stitches on the right-hand needle; bind the first stitch off over the second as usual.

Continue until all the pairs of stitches have been worked together and one stitch remains on the right-hand needle. Cut off the yarn, leaving a 6" tail. Enlarge the stitch remaining on the right-hand needle until the tail pulls through.

Note: *Bind off gently to avoid gathering the edge.*

Modified Conventional Bind-Off

This gives a looser edge and is faster and smoother to work (especially on a purl row) than the usual "lift stitch over" method. The knit version is a little trickier to learn as we are not used to putting the left-hand needle into a stitch before the right-hand needle!

On a Knit Row: Knit the first stitch as usual.

Diagram 25, knit the first stitch as usual.

*Slip the tip of the left-hand needle *purlwise* into the single new stitch on the right-hand needle, with the left-hand needle pointing towards the back of the work. See *Diagram 26 below.*

Diagram 26, left needle entering the new stitch purlwise.

Keeping the left-hand needle in the new stitch, put the tip of the right-hand needle knitwise into the next stitch to be worked on the left-hand needle (just as usual). See *Diagram 27.*

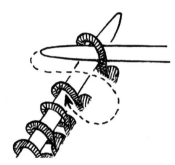

Diagram 27.

The right-hand needle should come out between the two stitches at the back of the needle. This creates an X formed by the two crossed stitches on the needles.

Throw the yarn as for a normal knit stitch and bring the loop out towards you through both stitches in turn, under the X formed by the two stitches. Allow both stitches just worked to drop off the left-hand needle. Repeat from *. See *Diagram 28.*

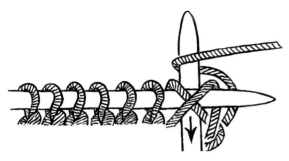

Diagram 28.

On a Purl Row: Purl the first stitch as usual.
** Slip the tip of the left-hand needle purlwise into the stitch on the right-hand needle; then slip the tip of the right-hand needle purlwise into the next stitch to be worked, p2t. Repeat from **.

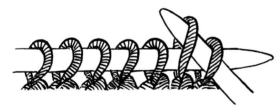

Diagram 29.

This is a regular bind-off and the resulting structure is identical. Whether binding off knitwise or purlwise the "new" right-hand stitch is always slipped *purlwise* onto the left-hand needle before engaging the next stitch to be worked in the usual manner. It makes a looser edge because

the outer stitch becomes stretched while you work the next one. The action of inserting the left needle into the new stitch before engaging the right needle takes some practice, but it is well worth the effort.

Tubular Bind-Off for 1 x 1 and 2 x 2 Rib

It is often difficult to satisfactorily bind-off toe-up socks as most bind-off methods restrict the elasticity of the fabric. Tubular needle-sewn methods can give pleasing rounded and elastic edges. A tubular edge is nothing more than a stocking stitch graft between the purl and knit stitches of the same round.

If you remove a needle from a piece of ribbing the stitches separate into two groups. The front group are the knit stitches and the rear ones the purls; it is these two layers that are joined together by the graft, stitch head to stitch head. A tubular bind-off can be made easier by working the last two rounds on larger-size needles or in addition, working the knit stitches only (slipping the purl stitches wyif) for one round, followed by the purl stitches only (slipping the knits wyib) before beginning the bind-off. For precise directions and diagrams please refer to *Reader's Digest Knitters' Handbook* by Montse Stanley.

Abbreviations

dpn(s)	Double-pointed needle(s). These may be rigid or flexible (circular) if you prefer.
inc	Increase by one stitch by the most appropriate method of your choice, such as RSI.
k2t	Knit two stitches together. This produces a one-stitch, right-slanting decrease.
kw	Knitwise; the needle enters the stitch as if to knit. A stitch when slipped knitwise changes its orientation on the needle, from the right-hand leg of the stitch lying in front to the left-hand leg in front. The orientation of the stitches involved in a decrease will affect the direction in which the decrease slopes. Always read the full decrease directions for exact details of any slipped stitches if you are in any doubt. Most decrease slips are kw. Slip a few stitches both knitwise and purlwise and examine the results. *See also pw.*
LHN	Left-hand needle.
LHS	Left-hand side.
m1	Make one stitch. Knit under the bar, before the next stitch.
O	Yarn over needle (as if to knit), to create a new stitch. When working into the "over" on the next row/round, the "over" should remain open and give a small decorative hole (or eyelet). If your "overs" close up, experiment with working into them differently or check the direction in which you throw the yarn for the "over."
p2t	Purl two stitches together to form one stitch decrease.
p3t	Purl three stitches together to form one stitch.
PCCO	Provisional Crochet Cast-On, *see page 110*.
pw	Purlwise; as if to purl (needle-tip to needle-tip). A stitch slipped purlwise doesn't change its orientation on the needle. Stitches are slipped purlwise unless otherwise specified, but those involved in a decrease are most commonly slipped knitwise; check the full decrease definition for precise details.

PWDD	Purlwise double decrease. With yarn in purl position, slip two stitches knitwise one at a time to the RHN, insert tip of LHN into the inner, then the outer, of the two slipped stitches and return them to the LHN, p3t. *The **knitwise** slipping alters the order of the stitches so that when the decrease (p3t) is made, it lies centrally about the middle stitch.*
RHN	Right-hand needle.
RHS	Right-hand side.
RS	Right side; the public side of the work.
RSI	Increase one stitch by knitting into the stitch below the next one waiting on the left needle. This produces a subtle, right-slanting increase; the easiest way to make this increase is to drop the tip of the right-hand needle from above, and at the back of the work, into the stitch head of the stitch below. With the right-hand needle in this position, marked x on the diagram below, throw the yarn as if to knit and draw the new loop through. To avoid puckering, give this new stitch a little extra slack, as it is emanating from the row below.

Ensure when making this increase that you knit only into the underneath stitch and not into both the underneath one and the one above it. There should only be one strand of yarn on the right-hand needle when you draw the new yarn through. If both stitches are worked together, a small hole will be created.

s1	Slip one stitch purlwise (unless otherwise stated) and unworked from left to right needle.
s1kw	Slip one stitch knitwise from left to right needle.

s2tkw-k1-psso
Slip two stitches together, knitwise, knit one more stitch, pass both previously slipped stitches over it.

st(s)
Stitch(es).

ssk
Slip the next two stitches, knitwise, one at a time, to the right-hand needle, insert the left-hand needle purlwise into the front of both slipped stitches from left to right and knit them together. This produces a one-stitch, left-slanting decrease known as a "Slip, slip, knit."

ssp
Slip the next two stitches knitwise, one at a time, to the right-hand needle, slip these two stitches back to the left-hand needle purlwise (needle-tip to needle-tip), now p2t (purl two together) through back of loops. This produces a one-stitch, left-slanting decrease when viewed from the right side, known as a "slip, slip, purl." If preferred, in the garter stitch toes and heels, a straightforward p2t may be substituted with very little outward difference.

SWR
Slip, wrap and replace. Slip the next stitch purlwise and unworked to the right-hand needle, bring the yarn between the needles, and then return the slipped stitch to the left-hand needle. Make this wrap of yarn around the stitch fairly firm. Subsequently, when working this wrapped stitch, leave the wrap *in situ* and work the stitch as usual. The purpose of wrapping the yarn around a stitch is to prevent the formation of holes; if you were to change the direction of knitting mid-row without wrapping the stitch beyond the turn, there would be a distinct gap at this point. When making wraps in garter stitch, there is no need to attend to the wrap later as it blends in with the garter bumps.

tbl
Through back of loop.

turn
Turn the knitting around and work in the opposite direction, although unworked stitches remain on the left-hand needle at this point. Incomplete rows such as these are also known as "short rows."

W	Wrap. Lay a piece of WY over the Main yarn at the edge of the work, before knitting the first stitch of the new row. (In this situation, a fine WY is best.) Knit the new row as usual with the Main yarn. Ignore the WY now trapped at the side. The resulting blip (or wrap) of Main yarn around the WY is the exact spot where the yarn changes direction at the end of each row. It will later be used as a mock stitch into which to knit-up new stitches. Do not leave any extra slack in the edge stitches. The wrap should be quite snug around the WY. *See Diagram 5 page 30.*
WS	Wrong side; the private side of the work. For your eyes only!
WY	Waste yarn; used to hold stitches temporarily and later removed. The yarn chosen should be smooth (easy to unravel and unlikely to leave stray fibers behind), of a similar weight to the Main yarn (to prevent distortion of the stitches of either yarn), and brightly contrasting (for maximum visibility and easy stitching).
wyib	With yarn in back, away from the knitter, ready to knit.
wyif	With yarn in front, towards the knitter, ready to purl.
yfw	Yarn forward. Bring yarn forward toward the knitter.

Many of the techniques described in Lucy's patterns are demonstrated on her **Knitter's Companion** series of DVDs! Ask your local yarn store or visit www.lucyneatby.com

Bibliography

Anatolian Knitting Designs, Betsy Harrell, Redhouse, Istanbul, 1981

And A Time to Knit Stockings, Katherine Pence, Pence Design Works, 1997

Bauerliches Stricken 1 - 3, Lisl Fanderl, Rosenheimer, 1975-83

Designs for Knitting Kilt Hose & Knickerbocker Stockings, Veronica Gainford, Schoolhouse Press, 1978, 1995

Easy Toe-Up Socks, Katherine Foster, 2001

Ethnic Socks and Stockings, Priscilla A. Gibson-Roberts, XRX, 1995

Fancy Feet, Anna Zilboorg, Lark Press, 1994

Folk Socks, Nancy Bush, Interweave Press, 1994

Folk Knitting in Estonia, Nancy Bush, Interweave Press, 1999

The Fun Sock, Maie and Taiu Landra, Koigu Wool Designs, 1998

The Handknitted Christmas Stocking Book, Edward Myatt, 1993, 1994

Homespun, Handknit, Linda Ligon, Interweave Press, 1987

Knitting for Anarchists, Anna Zilborg, Feet on the Ground Press, 2002

Knitting on the Road, Nancy Bush, Interweave Press, 2001

Latvian Dreams, Joyce Williams, Schoolhouse Press, 2000

Legs for Easy Toe Up Socks, Katherine Foster

The Magic Loop, Bev Galeskas and Sarah Hauschka, Fiber Trends, 2002

Reader's Digest Knitter's Handbook, Montse Stanley, Reader's Digest, 1986, 1993

Ribbing Plain and Fancy, Joy Slayton, Joy Knits, 1996

Simple Socks Plain and Fancy, Priscilla A. Gibson-Roberts, Nomad Press, 2001

Socks, Spin-Off Magazine, Interweave Press, 1994

Socks, Socks, Socks, Knitter's Magazine, XRX, 1999

Socks for Sandals & Clogs, Anna Zilboorg, Feet on the Ground Press, 1999

Socks Soar on Circular Needles, Cat Bordi, Passing Paws Press, 2001

The Twisted Sisters Sock Workbook, Lynne Vogel, Interweave Press, 2002

Index

Lucy Neatby

"Become the yarn! *Think* like a piece of yarn!"
That is the innovative advice knitting-design guru Lucy Neatby shares with her students in her popular knitting classes throughout Canada and the United States. And it works! When knitters take that advice to heart and also take charge of the technicalities of their craft, they can achieve whatever they set their hearts on.

Once a qualified Navigating Officer in the British Merchant Navy, Lucy plied at least five of the seven seas, knitting as she went. Then she found herself beached ashore in Wales, married to another mariner and within a few years, the mother of three charming children. To keep her sanity amidst the diapers and drudgery, she did much elaborate knitting when the children slept.

A few years later, the family moved to Nova Scotia, Canada. No sooner did Lucy arrive on the new continent than she set out to boldly go and knit things never knit before. Soon she was capitalising on her knitting expertise, acquired in "the School of Unravelling," by teaching classes and designing, first one pattern, then several.

Tradewind Knitwear Designs (so called in happy homage to Lucy's nautical past), now boasts more than 80 of Lucy's patterns and kits, along with favoured knitting supplies, DVD's with Lucy's innovative knitting techniques along with a companion DVD for this book, a catalogue, a fetching website, and a full mail-order service. Truth to tell, Tradewind is rapidly outgrowing the original dining room workspace, the kitchen and even the basement family room!

Corrie Watt

Lucy can be reached through her website:
> www.lucyneatby.com
> Toll Free: 1 866 272-7796
> Fax: 1 902 434-0345

Or write to her at:
> Tradewind Knitwear Designs Inc.
> 45 Dorothea Drive,
> Dartmouth, NS
> B2W 5X4   Canada

For wholesale orders, please contact Lucy directly.

Heart Garland

Make a sweet string of hearts in cheerful colors.

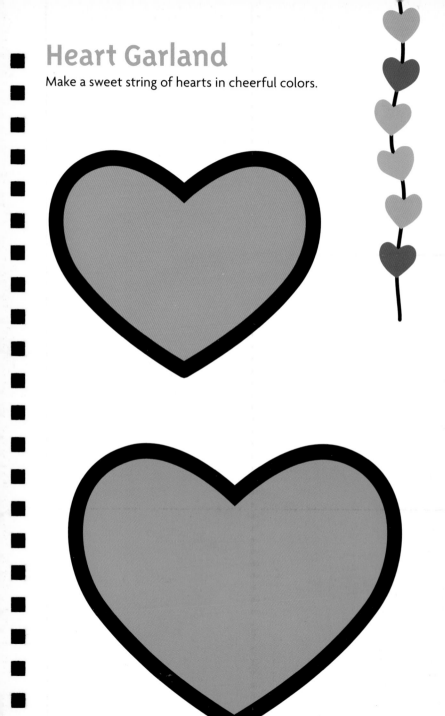

Outer Space Garland

Create a whole galaxy of planets, stars, and moons!

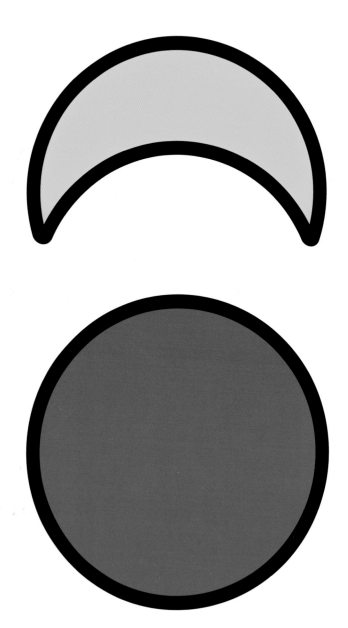

Garden Garland

Mix and match colors to make a pretty climbing vine.

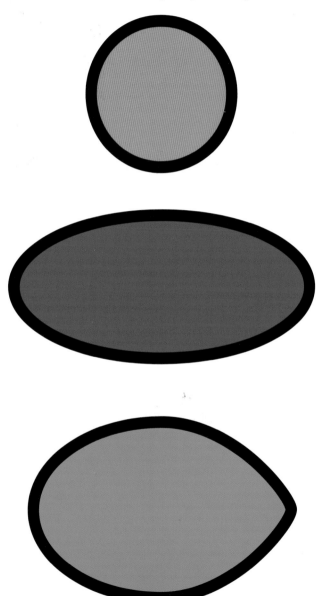

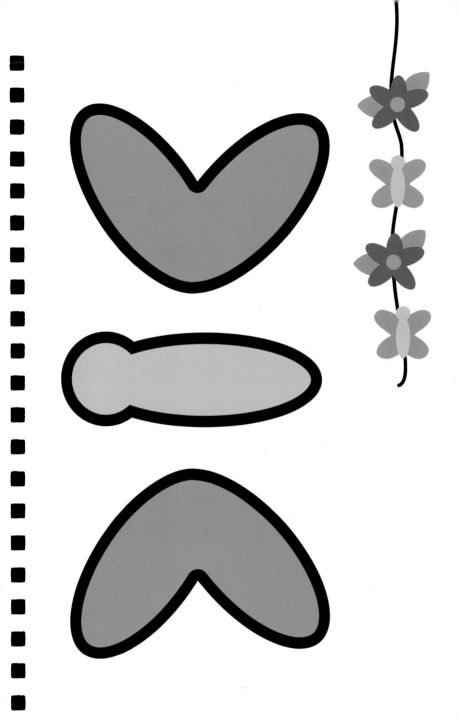

57

Kite Garland

Make a high-flying kite with a cute, contrasting tail.

giggle page

What do bumblebees chew?
Bumble gum!

Where's the best place to hide a chocolate?
In your mouth!

Why don't leopards play hide-and-seek?
Because they're always spotted!

When is a girl's dress like a frog?
When it's a jumper!

Where does a polar bear keep its money?
In a snowbank!

Knock knock.
Who's there?
Pasture.
Pasture who?
Pasture bedtime, isn't it?

What's the difference between a teacher and a train?
A teacher says, "Spit out your gum."
A train says, "Chew, chew!"

Ha-ha-ha! Hee-hee-hee! Ha-ha-ha! Hee-hee-hee!

parent checklist

Phone number where parents can be reached:

Address and phone number of house you're in:

Nearest intersection of house you're in:

Name and phone number of a neighbor:

Children's food and medicine allergies, if any:

Emergency numbers:

welcome home!

Here's what we did while you were out:

Movies or TV shows we watched:

Foods we ate:

Books we read:

Games we played:

Crafts we made:

Bedtimes:

Other things you should know:

notes for next time

What I want to remember from *this* time:

Kids' names and ages:

What I brought with me:

What I'll bring next time:

What we did:

How the kids acted:

What worked:

What didn't work so well:

Care to share a game or activity from your own Super Sitter's Playbook?

Write to

Babysitting Editor
American Girl
8400 Fairway Place
Middleton, WI 53562

All comments and suggestions received by American Girl may be used without compensation or acknowledgment. Sorry—photos can't be returned.

Here are some other American Girl books you might like:

Discover online games, quizzes, activities,
and more at **americangirl.com**